ACCESS TO JUSTICE FOR DISADVANTAGED COMMUNITIES

Marjorie Mayo, Gerald Koessl, Matthew Scott
and Imogen Slater

First published in Great Britain in 2015 by

Policy Press
University of Bristol
1-9 Old Park Hill
Bristol BS2 8BB
UK
t: +44 (0)117 954 5940
e: pp-info@bristol.ac.uk
www.policypress.co.uk

North American office:
Policy Press
c/o The University of Chicago Press
1427 East 60th Street
Chicago, IL 60637, USA
t: +1 773 702 7700
f: +1 773-702-9756
e:sales@press.uchicago.edu
www.press.uchicago.edu

British Library Cataloguing in Publication Data
A catalogue record for this book is available from the British Library

Library of Congress Cataloging-in-Publication Data
A catalog record for this book has been requested

ISBN 978-1-4473-1105-8 paperback

Cover design by Policy Press
Front cover image: Charlotte Berger
Printed and bound in Great Britain by
Marston Book Services Ltd, Oxfordshire
Policy Press uses environmentally responsible print partners

To the memory of Julia Burdett, who sadly died before she could complete her work on the research that informs this book, and to all those who continue to strive for Justice for All.

Contents

Acknowledgements

We would like to express our warmest appreciation and thanks to all those who have participated in the research, giving so generously of their time despite all the other pressures on them over this period. In particular we should also like to thank our Advisory Committee members, who were an invaluable source of advice and support throughout the project. The Law Centres Federation (now the Law Centres Network) was a similarly invaluable source of advice. Special thanks are due to those who very kindly gave detailed feedback on earlier drafts of the research report and to those who very kindly gave detailed comments on the final version for this book.

We should also like to acknowledge the administrative support that we have received from Goldsmiths, University of London throughout the research period and subsequently as we revised the research report for wider publication.

Warmest appreciation goes to colleagues at Policy Press and to the anonymous reader whose feedback has been extremely helpful. Any remaining errors and shortcomings are, of course, down to us.

Finally, and most importantly, we would like to thank the Leverhulme Trust for its unfailing support during the course of the research.

Abbreviations and glossary

Best Value	Introduced in England and Wales in 1999 by the Labour government, a policy to improve local services in terms of both quality and cost, seeking continuous improvement, and combining economy, efficiency and effectiveness.
CAB	Citizens Advice Bureau
Carter reforms	Reforms proposed by Lord Carter (2006) and implemented in 2007, focusing on changes to legal aid as explained in Chapter Two.
CLAC	Community Legal Advice Centre
CLAN	Community Legal Advice Network
commissioning	The process by which government departments and local authorities secure their services, usually through a legal procurement process.
commodification	The assignment of economic value to something not previously considered in economic terms.
decommodification	In this context, the protection of citizens from market forces (associated with welfare state services provided on the basis of need rather than the ability to pay).
de-professionalisation	A 'condition' in which professional autonomy and scope for the exercise of judgement – among other defining characteristics of a professional – become undermined.
fixed fee	A fixed price for each piece of work, in contrast to legal charges accruing according to time spent.
LASPO	Legal Aid, Sentencing and Punishment of Offenders Act (2012)
Law Society	The representative body for solicitors in England and Wales.
LCF	Law Centres Federation (subsequently Law Centres Network)
legal aid	Government funding to help with the costs of legal advice for people who cannot afford it.
LSC	Legal Services Commission
Management Committee	The committee with responsibility for providing strategic direction to Law Centres (usually made up of some combination of community representatives and those with relevant professional skills). Management Committee members may also be trustees (see below), although they may not all have the specific responsibilities associated with being a trustee.
modernisation	The government's strategy to reform and update public services.
NEF	New Economics Foundation
neoliberalism	A contemporary political philosophy advocating economic liberalisation, open markets, and emphasising the role of the private sector.
New Right	A strand of Conservatism developed in the UK in the early 1980s, also associated with Thatcherism (Margaret Thatcher).
NHS	National Health Service
New Public Management	An approach prominent since the 1980s, based on the premise that market-oriented management of the public sector will lead to greater cost efficiency and improved service delivery.

public legal education	Training that equips people with knowledge and skills to identify and tackle law-related problems.
pro bono	*Pro bono publico* translates from Latin as 'for the public good': in the legal profession this term refers to lawyers providing services free, on a voluntary basis, to those who are unable to afford them.
QC	Queen's Counsel, a lawyer appointed by letters patent to be one of her Majesty's Counsel.
recommodification	Returning to the private market the provision of goods or services that had previously been provided publicly (eg via privatisation)
stakeholder	A person, group or organisation that has a direct or indirect stake in an organisation, partnership or similar endeavour.
trades council	An association of labour unions or branches in a given geographical area.
trustees	The name that charity law uses to define the group of people who have ultimate responsibility for an organisation that is a recognised charity: they may also be called the Management Committee, Directors, Executive Committee and so on.
Unified Contract	The Unified Contract for civil legal aid providers (2007) replaced the General Civil Contract and Family Mediation Contract. It brought conditions for not-for-profit advisors into line with those of solicitors who carried out civil legal aid work.
VCO	voluntary and community organisation

Introduction: accessing social justice in disadvantaged communities

This book explores the dilemmas being faced by professionals and volunteers who are aiming to provide access to justice for all and to promote social justice agendas in increasingly challenging contexts. Public service **modernisation**[1] has been accompanied by increasing marketisation and massive public expenditure cuts, with escalating effects in terms of the growth of social inequalities. As the following chapters illustrate, Law Centres have provided a lens through which to examine the implications of these wider policies, as increasing marketisation has been impacting upon staff and volunteers working to promote social justice in disadvantaged communities.

Given their underpinning ethos and missions, Law Centres offer particular insights into the tensions inherent in increasing marketisation, against a background of public service modernisation agendas more generally. Although they have been valuable as a means of exploring these issues, Law Centres have been relatively under-researched in the past, and so they have provided a relatively fresh context within which to investigate experiences of these wider issues and potential tensions.

Social justice has been a central public policy theme, from the discussions that led up to the development of post-war welfare state reforms in Britain through to more recent debates on social welfare and social justice in contemporary Britain. 'Everybody is in favour of social justice', it has been argued, even if 'what they mean by social justice, the priority they accord to it, relative to other objectives, and the public policies they believe follow from it, vary widely' (Burchardt and Craig, 2008, p 1). 'Although few say they agree with injustice', as Dorling points out, 'nevertheless we live in an unjust world' (Dorling, 2010, p 1).

The welfare state has itself been the subject of continuing debate since that time, and particularly so in recent years as successive governments have developed strategies to promote public service reforms, significantly changing the respective roles to be played by the state, civil society and the private market. Increasing the use of market mechanisms has been presented as a central plank of public service modernisation. This has not only been advocated as a means of ensuring value for money in times of public expenditure constraint (although that clearly has been a central concern); the increased use of market mechanisms has, in addition, been presented as a mechanism for promoting user choice, putting the consumer rather than the producers of welfare in the driving seat.

According to a range of critics, this strategy would, it was argued, address concerns with the rigidities and unresponsiveness of state bureaucracies and the manifestations of professional self-interest and paternalistic control that were distorting public welfare provision. Privatisation was, according to former Prime Minister Margaret Thatcher, at 'the centre of reclaiming territory for freedom', a means by which 'the state's power is reduced and the power of the people enhanced' (Thatcher, 1993, p 676). For New Labour, the increasing use of market mechanisms (although without necessarily involving privatisation per se) was similarly central to public service reform. As then Prime Minister Tony Blair explained, this was because competitive pressures and incentives drive up quality, efficiency and responsiveness in the public sector (Blair, 2001), with 'diversity of supply' and choice in place of the 'old practices' (Blair, 2002, in Seldon, 2004, p 634). The resulting more commercial modes of operation and reorientation towards the service user as consumer have resulted in what has been described as 'a transcendent restructuring of the public sector that has cultural, ideological and institutional dimensions' (Doonan, 2009, p 140).

The policy outcomes that have ensued from increasing marketisation have had significant implications in terms of social justice in general and access to justice more specifically, posing increasing challenges and dilemmas for those involved in providing legal services in disadvantaged communities. These tensions have been central to wider debates about social welfare and the future of the welfare state, overall. Access to justice has been valued as a right in itself, as well as representing a means of accessing other rights such as welfare rights. This had been a central plank in post-war debates on the significance of establishing a framework for providing **legal aid** as part of the development of the welfare state more generally.

In the context of contemporary policy debates, the question of access to justice has gained additional significance. Public service modernisation strategies have emphasised the importance of having informed consumers, aware of and competent in making choices and accessing rights and services. But without effective access to legal information and advocacy, people – especially people from disadvantaged communities, whether geographically defined in terms of disadvantaged neighbourhoods or communities based upon shared identities or concerns – risk being effectively deprived of such options. Access to legal aid has become increasingly relevant, then, facilitating choices and enabling citizens to obtain their welfare rights, challenging bureaucratic and professional decision making where necessary (arguably more necessary than ever, in fact, in a period of rapid legislative change with major impacts in terms of social welfare rights).

Within these debates on access to justice and the provision of legal aid, over past decades Law Centres have occupied a particular place. This is because, from the 1970s, Law Centres developed their approaches to the provision of legal services on the basis of particular concepts of justice and access to justice, involving the need for advocacy and campaigning for the rights of people from disadvantaged communities. Drawing upon models developed in the US and elsewhere, Law Centres were established with remits that went way beyond the provision of legal services to individuals who were unable to afford such services through the private market. From the 1960s, in addition to meeting the legal needs of individual clients, the US War on Poverty had provided for legal services that could take up test cases and pursue class actions, challenging the causes of injustice and inequality (Johnson, 1999), campaigning for changing 'governmental systems when they adversely affected the poor' (Kilwein, 1999, p 46). There should be community involvement, it was argued, with active support for citizen groups that were seeking to empower that community, if these strategies for social change were to be effective in promoting greater justice for the poor.

This model extended the concept of justice way beyond the notion of equality of treatment, recognising the limits to such an approach, given the fundamental inequalities that were inherent in so many Western democratic societies. These were not level playing fields. According to Bauman:

> One of the most notorious sore spots of democratic regimes is the contradiction between the formal universality of democratic rights (accorded to all citizens equally) and the less than universal ability of their holders to exercise such rights effectively; in other words, the gap separating the legal condition of a citizen '*de jure*' from the practical capacity of a citizen *de facto* – a gap expected to be bridged by individuals deploying their own skills and resources, which, however, they may – and in a huge number of cases do – lack. (Bauman, 2011, p 13)

As feminists and others concerned with social justice have similarly argued, equal treatment for all does not necessarily lead to equitable outcomes for all if structural inequalities such as those arising from gender, race, ethnicity and social class divisions remain unchallenged (Phillips, 2002; Young, 2008).

Race and ethnicity have been particularly significant factors here. Minorities have been subject to direct discrimination and they have been at risk of experiencing institutional racism. Particular communities have been disproportionately at risk of experiencing poverty, unemployment, homelessness and educational disadvantage, for example, just as they have been disproportionately at risk of experiencing poor physical and mental health outcomes (Craig et al, 2012). In addition, barriers of language and culture have impacted upon minority communities' opportunities for challenging discrimination and accessing rights, barriers that have been especially problematic for so many asylum seekers and refugees.

In line with the implications of this approach, the Law Centres' umbrella body, the Law Centres Network, explained that it was not only that 'Law Centres defend the legal rights of people who cannot afford a lawyer'; in addition, 'they are specialists working in their local communities to uphold justice and advance equality'. 'They are independent and directly accountable to the communities they serve through committees of local people', as is stated in the Network's annual report for 2010–11 (see www.law.centres.org.uk), emphasising the importance of community involvement and accountability together with the importance of undertaking **public legal education** and preventative work, pursuing test cases to challenge discrimination and to advance the cause of social justice more generally.

The research that has informed this book explored the experiences and dilemmas that these challenges of modernisation agendas were posing for professionals and volunteers. Were these policy agendas facilitating the development of new forms of professionalism, based on new forms of accountability to service users and communities, as the advocates of public service modernisation were suggesting? Was increasing marketisation an effective strategy for improving quality and choice as well as enhancing cost-effectiveness in Law Centres' provision of legal aid? Were service users being put in the driving seat, empowered to make choices and challenge bureaucratic structures and professional self-interests as informed consumers, as some academics and policy professionals have suggested (Le Grand, 2003)? Or conversely, were these policy agendas being experienced as promoting new forms of **de-professionalisation** and demoralisation (Banks, 2004), potentially undermining the occupational values and identities of those involved in public service provision, such as those involved in the work of Law Centres?

Were there alternative strategies that could be developed for public service reform, even within the constraints of the current policy framework, in this age of austerity? If, as Sandel, among others, has argued, there should be some things that money can't buy (Sandel, 2012), how might this shape public debates on what should be the limits of marketisation, with what potential outcomes for the public service ethos and for policies to promote equality and social justice (however defined) more widely? While focusing on professionals and volunteers in Law Centres concerned with the provision of access to justice, the research explored issues with resonance for wider debates on the future of public service professionals, the public service ethos and the wider welfare state. The appendices provide further details, explaining the research methodology and highlighting some of the research findings that provide evidence in support of arguments put forward in the main text.

The chapters that follow

Chapter One begins by examining the framework of earlier debates on social justice, social citizenship and the welfare state, exploring how these have framed subsequent debates. The contributions of Esping Andersen have particular relevance here. Like Titmuss and others before him, Esping Andersen pointed to the tensions inherent in policies to promote accountability and choice for service users – increasing choices for some, while effectively reducing choices for other individuals and communities less able to meet their needs through the private market for a variety of reasons, including the lack of information as well as the lack of money and other resources. Chapter One concludes by summarising recent debates on marketisation and on public service modernisation agendas more generally, including the potential impacts on public service professionals, the public service ethos, professional power and increasing – or decreasing – accountability to service users.

Chapter Two begins by focusing upon differing definitions of and perspectives on social justice, together with their varying implications for public policy. This sets the framework for the ensuing historical summary of public policies concerned with the promotion of access to justice and social citizenship for all, starting from earlier debates in the post-Second World War period.

In the event, the post-war welfare state settlement failed to realise the principle of equal access to the law in Britain, in practice leaving gaps that were subsequently taken up by radical lawyers and others. Drawing upon models developed in the US and elsewhere, these lawyers and their allies pressed for the development of the first Law Centres, within the context of wider pressures for rights and equalities in the late 1960s and early 1970s.

The chapter then moves on to examine the development of legal aid policies more recently, from the 1990s to the present time, including the changes to legal aid that have been the subject of legislation enacted in 2012.

Chapter Three moves on to consider debates on ethics and values, with a particular focus on the public service ethos and professional values. This sets the context for the discussion of Law Centres' own distinctive ethos and values. Law Centres were established with strong commitments to the values inherent in providing equal access to the law, regardless of the ability to pay and/or other social advantages and disadvantages, together with commitments to working with disadvantaged communities to promote social justice agendas more widely. In addition, Law Centres were typically committed to collective and collaborative ways of working, with strong community involvement, developing preventative work as well as working with individuals holistically. These goals were potentially challenging to achieve in practice at the best of times, let alone when teams were facing major external pressures for change as a result of increasing marketisation.

Chapter Four focuses more specifically on the challenges and dilemmas that have been facing Law Centre staff and volunteers, first with the introduction of the **Carter reforms** under New Labour (introducing competitive tendering for contracts and **fixed fees** for payment) and then with more recent threats to the provision of legal aid more generally. The chapter concludes by identifying key dilemmas that have been the subject of contemporary debates within and about Law Centres.

Chapter Five moves on to consider public service modernisation, restructuring and **recommodification**. One of the distinctive features of public service modernisation agendas has been the emphasis upon restructuring management and accountability systems, including the increasing use of performance targets rather than reliance upon previous accountability systems, including the collective ways of working and community accountability systems that had been typical features of many Law Centres. Collective ways of working fitted uneasily with the requirements of the Legal Services Commission, and in this context community involvement was becoming increasingly problematic.

There were, in addition, dilemmas surrounding staff pay and conditions of employment and the extent to which relatively favourable conditions could be maintained in the current post-2008 funding context. The chapter includes some discussion of pressures for restructuring the labour process itself, including concerns about the potential for deskilling among professionals through the increasing use of alternative and cheaper forms of labour.

Chapter Five concludes by focusing upon one of the most controversial dilemmas facing Law Centres in the context of increasing marketisation: the issue of charging clients. In the past, charging clients for services had been widely perceived as being in conflict with Law Centres' ethos and values. More recently, however, opinions have been shifting as Law Centre staff, **management committees/ trustees** and volunteers have been faced with the prospect that many of the legal aid services that were previously on offer might be lost altogether, presenting a dilemma to which there have been no comfortable answers.

Issues of conflict and competition versus collaboration, partnership working and planning are addressed in Chapter Six. Law Centres have experienced conflicts with other agencies in the past (when acting as advocates for clients, questioning professional decision making, for example, or challenging public bureaucracies such as local authorities over inadequate or inequitable service provision). More recently, pressures towards conflict and competition have been increasing. One of the distinctive features of public service modernisation agendas, and of marketisation agendas more generally, has been the pressure to compete – competition being assumed by governments to promote increasing efficiency and choice.

A number of Law Centres had already had some experience of competing with other agencies, such as Citizens Advice Bureaux, and other advice agencies, although there were also Law Centres that focused upon the importance of collaborative ways of working, aiming to provide holistic services to communities and working with other organisations and agencies where there were shared interests in policy and campaigning work. The funding system for legal aid that was introduced following the Carter reforms exacerbated existing tendencies towards competition as agencies bid against each other for contracts.

As Law Centres struggled to develop survival strategies, a number of them began to explore ways of collaborating rather than competing with other, like-minded agencies, aiming to provide coordinated services that were more user friendly as well as more cost-effective. In some cases these explorations were initiated, or at least supported, by funders such as local authorities who were keen to identify ways of making savings while meeting increasing needs for advice and advocacy services as a result of welfare reforms and public expenditure cuts.

Another distinguishing aspect of marketised labour processes relates to the issue of time and pressures on the use of time in order to maximise productivity. As E.P. Thompson has reflected, notions of time changed with the development of industrial capitalism, bringing new forms of work discipline and the management of time (Thompson, 1967). Such changes have continued in varying forms in more recent times. Chapter Seven explores these issues as they relate to Law Centres in the context of public service modernisation. The funding system that was associated with the Carter reforms mirrored private sector systems in that the time allotted to each client needed to be carefully monitored and controlled, in order to keep within the parameters approved for payment. This posed major dilemmas in many Law Centres aiming, as they typically did, to meet the needs of clients holistically, taking the time to listen to clients in disadvantaged communities who might be presenting a number of related problems, including problems with expressing themselves in English as a second language and/or as a result of having experienced mental health or other disempowering issues in their lives.

However, Law Centres' missions to work holistically and in preventative ways, with communities as well as with individuals, could be seen in terms of time valued and time well spent – making effective savings for the longer term through preventative policy work – rather than in terms of time wasted. A number of staff contrasted what they saw as the real value of time spent working in such ways with clients and communities with the time that was, in their view, being wasted as a result of cumbersome bureaucratic requirements, together with the time wasted as a result of poor decision making in public bodies, leading to the need for subsequent appeals. Time pressures have emerged, then, as a major set of challenges and dilemmas.

Chapter Eight draws together evidence on the impact of these challenges and dilemmas in terms of staff motivation and commitment. One of the criticisms that has been levelled at **New Public Management** systems is that they presuppose negative views of human motivation, assuming that employees in general, and professionals more specifically, need the discipline of targets imposed from above so as to ensure that they do not operate in self-interested ways. Conversely, critics of the New Public Management have argued that target-type cultures actually risk alienating public service workers, undermining the very motivations and commitments that brought them into the public service professions in the first place.

The chapter provides examples of disaffection and demoralisation among Law Centre staff. There were indications too that some of those coming into Law Centres more recently were less clearly committed to Law Centres' espoused ethos and values – volunteers, for example, who came to Law Centres as students or recently qualified law graduates in order to gain experience and so enhance their employability in difficult times. What did not emerge, however, was evidence of any widespread tendency for the next generation of staff and volunteers to embrace more marketised values. There is evidence, on the contrary, that some of the next generation have actually developed a strengthened commitment to public service-type values as a direct result of their experiences in Law Centres. And there is plenty of evidence to testify to the continuing commitment of those staff and volunteers, including volunteer members of management committees/ trustees, who are giving of their time as a 'labour of love', facing dilemmas that would be considerably less taxing for them personally, were they not investing so much emotional labour in the process.

Chapter Nine reflects back on the starting points, the implications for access to justice for disadvantaged communities and the potentially wider implications for strategies for social justice, social citizenship and social welfare. The case for the continuing public resourcing of Law Centres is argued, together with the case for public support for advice and advocacy services more generally.

Meanwhile, Law Centres face continuing dilemmas in the face of increasing marketisation; dilemmas that have resonances across the provision of welfare services. What should be the limits to the role of the market? How far can alternative strategies to safeguard and further improve public services be developed in ways that strengthen rather than undermine the basic values and principles of public service provision? And, most importantly, how far can such survival strategies strengthen the position of those who need, as well as those who provide, public services, empowering communities to work more effectively with progressive organisations and groups in the wider pursuit of social justice agendas?

Note
[1] Where terms that are explained in the Glossary appear in the text for the first time they appear in bold type.

ONE

Social justice and the welfare state

Before exploring the role of the law, and access to legal advice and advocacy as the background to the study of Law Centres, this chapter summarises the framework of earlier debates (Marshall, 1950; Titmuss, 1968) on social citizenship and the welfare state. How did some of these debates conceptualise public policy interventions to promote social rights such as rights to education, health, welfare and social security, and what were the implications for access to justice? These approaches have been challenged from differing perspectives over time, as the chapter illustrates, setting the context for more recent debates as these relate to subsequent chapters. The chapter concludes by summarising recent debates on marketisation and on public service modernisation agendas more generally, and their potential impacts on public service professionals. This sets the framework for the discussion of social justice and the provision of legal aid in the following chapter.

Social justice and the origins of the post-war welfare state

Even before the end of the Second World War, access to justice figured in discussions about how to build upon previous welfare reforms. As Baroness Hale pointed out in her Sir Henry Hodge Memorial Lecture for the **Law Society** in 2011, 'when the [post-war] Welfare State was established in the United Kingdom after the Second World War, a legal aid and advice scheme was an important part of it' (Hale, 2011, p 6). She quoted E.J. Cohn, who wrote in 1943 that

> Legal aid is a service which the modern state owes its citizens as a matter of principle ... Just as the modern State tries to protect the poorer classes against the common dangers of life, such as unemployment, disease, old age, social oppression, etc., so it should protect them when legal difficulties arise. Indeed the case for such protection is stronger than the case for any other form of protection. The State is not responsible for the outbreak of epidemics, for old age or economic crises. But the State is responsible for the law. (Cohn, 1943)

This emphasis upon social protection was central to the thinking behind the 1942 Beveridge Report, with its emphasis upon identifying the major causes of, and so preventing, poverty and social distress (through state-organised insurance schemes to provide pensions, sickness and unemployment benefits, for example). The National Health Service (NHS) was established in this period, and was underpinned by similar approaches to the role of the state in meeting the needs of its citizens. Beveridge himself actually assumed a wider view of the state's responsibilities than did Cohn, recognising that the post-war welfare state settlement that was being established would depend upon full employment, a situation that, it was widely believed, the state could ensure through Keynesian economic policies.

According to the sociologist T.H. Marshall (1950), the post-war settlement represented a new relationship between citizens and the state. In the past, citizenship first had been defined in terms of the civil rights that were achieved in the eighteenth century, and then in terms of political rights too (with the extension of the right to vote to all citizens, including women, by the early twentieth century). The third phase, according to T.H. Marshall, extended the concept of citizenship still further, to include social rights and responsibilities by virtue of a person's being a citizen entitled to welfare. Discussing these social rights, he included the example of the (then) Legal Aid Bill, 'which offers a social service designed to strengthen the civil right of the citizen to settle his disputes in a court of law' (Marshall, 1950, p 48).

This emphasis on rights was also central to the thinking of other influential thinkers of the post-war period, including Titmuss, the author of a number of seminal publications on social welfare and the state. For Titmuss, one of the key characteristics of the welfare state was that services should be provided 'as social rights, on criteria of the *needs* of specific categories, groups and territorial areas and not dependent on *individual tests of* means' (Titmuss, 1968, p 122). The state must provide an infrastructure of universal services, he argued, promoting values of equality, freedom and social integration rather than simply providing residual (and implicitly second class) services for the poor, to be provided on the basis of discretion rather than on the basis of entitlement as of right.

These approaches have attracted controversy, however, and have been subject to criticisms from varying political positions over time. Titmuss himself was only too aware of the importance of addressing criticisms from the Left, as poverty and discrimination persisted, despite the welfare state, and were problems that were becoming increasingly evident by the mid to late 1960s (Abel-Smith and Townsend, 1965; Townsend, 1979). Titmuss was also concerned to address the increasingly evident failures to meet the needs of black and minority ethnic communities (although he was less focused on addressing feminist criticisms of the paternalistic ways in which services were being planned and delivered; Williams, 1989). But he was particularly concerned to challenge the criticisms of the Right, including those of Milton Friedman, whose influence has continued to have an impact with the rise of **neoliberal** approaches from the 1980s onward.

As Titmuss summarised the argument (Titmuss, 1968), Friedman and others of the Chicago School of Economics argued that, because societies were becoming richer (the assumption of that time being that UK, like other Western democracies, would continue to experience economic growth), the vast majority of their populations would be in a position to satisfy their own welfare needs in the private market without the help of the state. So they should have the freedom to make their own choices, expressing their own preferences and priorities. Titmuss disagreed. He argued that economic growth per se would not solve the problem of poverty, nor would private markets in welfare solve the problems of discrimination and stigma (associated with residual approaches to welfare provision).

In particular, Titmuss challenged Friedman's assumption that private markets in welfare offer consumers more choice, illustrating his argument with the example of private occupational pensions, which offered employees little control, let alone full transferability if workers moved jobs (and little in the way of guaranteed security, as has become only too apparent more recently). Finally, and most importantly, Titmuss challenged Friedman's assumption that social services, including medical care, have no characteristics that differentiate them from goods in the private market, pointing out that consumers were not necessarily in a position to make informed choices, nor could inadequate services simply be returned, like faulty goods, to the place of purchase. On the contrary, poor health choices – or indeed poor educational choices – could have life-long consequences for the unfortunate ill-informed consumer. The poorest and least informed citizens would be precisely those who could be expected to be most disadvantaged in terms of making such choices, or indeed accessing their rights at all.

In a subsequent book, *The gift relationship: From human blood to social policy*, Titmuss explored these arguments further, drawing upon comparative research on the procurement of human blood for medical purposes (Titmuss, 1970). As he demonstrated on the basis of evidence from the US, South Africa, the then USSR and elsewhere, paying 'donors' to provide blood was less effective than the British system of relying on genuinely voluntary donations, in terms both of the quantity and – most importantly – of the quality of the blood provided. There were a number of reasons for this, including the social characteristics of many of those 'donating' for commercial reasons.

'As a market transaction, information that might have a bearing on the quality of blood is withheld if possible from the buyer; such information could be detrimental to the price or the sale' (Titmuss, 1970, p 76), he argued, pointing to the difficulties of screening out 'donors' such as drug addicts, alcoholics and carriers of hepatitis, malaria and other diseases who were motivated to donate by the need for money to buy food and other necessities of life. In the US, for example, paid 'donors' included a category of 'professional donors', disproportionately likely to be poor, unskilled, unemployed and black: 'an exploited human population of high blood yielders'. 'Redistribution', Titmuss continued, 'in terms of the "gift of blood and blood products" from the poor to the rich appears to be one of the dominant effects of the American blood banking system' (Titmuss, 1970, p 119).

Once market mechanisms had been introduced into the procurement of blood, there was evidence to demonstrate the challenges of reverting to a voluntary system, such as the blood transfusion service that was being operated via the NHS in Britain at that time. It was, Titmuss argued, 'easier for societies to abandon altruism as a motive for giving blood than it is to abandon the principles of economic man once they have been institutionalized and accepted' (Titmuss,

1970, p 187). Commercialisation was both inefficient and socially inequitable, in other words (the poorest being most likely to 'donate' blood but least likely to be able to pay for it, should they need it themselves at some future date).

Most importantly, Titmuss concluded, commercialisation undermined altruistic motivation in society, the motivation to give to strangers for the well-being of the whole community. This was an ethical issue of central concern more generally, he concluded, arguing that social policy should be 'centred in those institutions that create integration and discharge alienation' (Titmuss, 1970, p 212). This was in no way to suggest that altruistic volunteering should be put forward as a substitute for publicly provided welfare but, rather, to argue that the welfare state should itself be promoting values of reciprocity and social solidarity in the wider society. The ethical implications of Titmuss's writings re-emerge in later chapters of this book.

There are parallels here with more recent debates on what the limits of markets should be. 'Do we want a society where everything is up for sale? Or are there certain moral and civic goods that markets do not honour and money cannot buy?' (Sandel, 2012, p 203).

More recent debates

These debates have continued in varying forms as subsequent governments have addressed the question of the balance between public and private provision in the field of social welfare. Among the work of more recent theorists, Esping Andersen's *The three worlds of welfare capitalism* (Esping Andersen, 1990) has particular relevance, with his theorisation of **decommodification**, building on T.H. Marshall's approach to developing the view that social citizenship constituted the core idea of the welfare state. Esping Andersen argued that removing or (more realistically) reducing the influence of market forces has been a significant distinguishing feature of social democratic approaches to social welfare. Rather than envisaging welfare services as goods to be bought and sold as commodities according to market-led criteria, he argued the case for 'decommodifying' welfare services so that services could be provided on the basis of need rather than of ability to pay for them in the private market. This was vitally important in terms of enabling citizens to access services that they might otherwise struggle to afford, leaving the poorest without effective access to basic services such as healthcare.

Even more importantly, Esping Andersen went on to argue, decommodifying services was also significant in terms of strengthening the bargaining power of working people more generally, rather than stigmatising them. In this approach he was including the ways in which facilitating access to education, for example, could strengthen the position of the less-powerful in society, enabling them to bargain more effectively for social rights and for social justice agendas more generally. There would seem to be parallels here with Amartya Sen's discussion of capabilities, the notion that people need particular capabilities, such as the capabilities provided by access to education, to put them in a position to effectively access their formal rights and freedoms (Sen, 1993).

Esping Andersen contrasted this broadly social democratic approach to the provision of welfare (as developed in Scandinavian countries in the past, for example) with other models. These included the corporatist model as developed in Germany, for example (based upon partnerships between the state, the corporate sector and other providers, including faith-based organisations). And they included the more liberal, market-orientated approaches that have characterised the provision of welfare in countries such as the US, and increasingly in Britain too.

Like Titmuss and others before him, Esping Andersen pointed to the tensions inherent in policies designed to promote choice – increasing choices for some while effectively reducing choices for other individuals and communities less able to meet their needs through the private market for a variety of reasons, including the lack of information and of other resources. Education is a case in point here, the provision of increasing choice for some parents and their children – through the provision of selective schools – having knock-on effects that reduce choice for others. As Titmuss had earlier pointed out, some people's welfare might result in other people's 'ill fare' (Abel-Smith and Titmuss, 1974). Social policies driven by private insurance interests, for example, risked being 'imposed without democratic discussion; without consideration of the moral consequences which may result from them' (Titmuss, 1960, p 2).

Neoliberalism and more recent policy developments

In more recent publications Esping Andersen developed his critique of the case for privatisation and deregulation (Esping Andersen, 1999; Esping Andersen et al, 2002), contrasting Swedish approaches (developed previously, before more recent policy shifts towards increasing privatisation) with US approaches. Increased use of the private sector shifted costs, rather than reducing expenditure completely, he argued, and the outcomes were increasingly unequal, leading him to the conclusion that 'A strategy based purely on deregulation and privatization cannot, like the American example shows, be welfare and efficient optimizing' (Esping Andersen, 1999, p 178).

But Britain was moving in the US direction, he suggested:

> Rather than tame, regulate, or marginalize markets so as to ensure human welfare, the idea [of the 'Third Way' under New Labour] is to adapt and empower citizens so that they may be far better equipped to satisfy their welfare needs within the market. At its core, it is a supply-driven policy attempting to furnish citizens with the requisites needed for individual success. Hence its flagship policies are training and lifelong learning. The assumption seems to be that the social risks and class inequalities that emanate from markets can be overridden if we target policy so that all compete on a more equal footing. (Esping Andersen et al, 2002, p 5)

Enabling people to compete with each other does not necessarily tackle structural inequalities, though. On the contrary, in fact, where structural inequalities have persisted, the outcomes have remained similarly unequal. And as later chapters illustrate, individuals and communities in deprived situations have been precisely those who have most needed support if they were to access their rights, let alone to claim new rights, as active and empowered citizens.

Left, feminist and anti-racist critics of the welfare state such as Williams (Williams, 1989) responded to these shifts towards the more neoliberal approaches that Esping Andersen was critiquing by arguing that, for all its faults and concessions to dominant interests, the welfare state still represented an 'important challenge by the working class to the social relations of capitalism – to get the state to safeguard the working class against the deleterious effects of capitalism' (Williams, 1989, p 205). There were parallels here with earlier arguments about the welfare state as representing significant gains in terms of equality and social justice (Wedderburn, 1965), whatever its limitations in practice (London Edinburgh Weekend Return, 1980). As the welfare state came under increasing attack, Williams argued that an integrated strategy was needed, not merely to defend past gains but to promote an alternative to that being promoted by the **New Right**, with new concepts of social justice and egalitarianism 'which embody class, "race" and gender interests' (Williams, 1989, p xvi).

In addition to challenges about costs (the argument that public spending on welfare was too high, but still increasing and so in need of control), criticisms of the welfare state were also focusing upon the issue of bureaucratic paternalism (Lee and Raban, 1988). Bureaucratic and professional paternalism (the so-called 'nanny state') had been a major concern of critics from the right of the political spectrum, but critics from the left were increasingly expressing similar concerns. What was needed was an 'agenda for empowerment', defined in terms of an 'empowerment-as-citizen' approach (Deakin, 1993, p 105) rather than in terms of individual consumerism – Deakin being very aware of the importance of defining such a slippery term (Lister, 1996; Beresford and Turner, 1997). Welfare states needed to be considered in terms of 'how' as well as of 'how much' welfare they provided, not simply in terms of the amount of services that were being provided through the private market or via decommodified systems, it was argued (Bonoli, 1997). This would add another dimension to Esping Andersen's 'three worlds of welfare capitalism' (Bonoli, 1997), taking account of services' accountability to service users and communities and their varying needs, whether these services were being provided through the public, private or voluntary community sectors. As Deakin (1993) had already pointed out, bureaucratic and professional paternalism could be combated in different ways and there *were* alternatives to the market-led agendas that had become increasingly prevalent by that time, in the early 1990s. The predominant policy response in Britain, however, was to promote precisely such market-led agendas.

Marketisation and public service modernisation

There is an extensive literature on neoliberal approaches to social welfare. It includes specific literatures on privatisation as well as specific literatures on the increasing role for market mechanisms within public and voluntary/not-for-profit sectors along with the increasing adoption of private sector approaches to management in these sectors (Finlayson, 2003; Page, 2007; Powell, 2008). The intention here is simply to summarise those aspects with particular relevance for later chapters, focusing upon the implications for public service professionals and volunteers such as those involved with Law Centres.

As the previous section has already summarised, New Right governments promoted policies to roll back the state with a view to enabling the market to operate more effectively, arguing that this offered individuals and their families more choice. Welfare provision was to be determined on the basis of rational consumer choices rather than being determined by paternalistic professionals and public sector bureaucrats deciding what was best for people – the 'nanny state'. Through the introduction of market mechanisms – 'quasi-markets' as Le Grand and colleagues initially characterised the processes by which 'monopolistic state providers' were to be replaced with 'competitive independent ones' (Le Grand and Bartlett, 1993, p 10) – welfare provision was to be transformed.

The key questions to be addressed, it was argued, were whether these changes would result in greater efficiency and cost savings or would prevent sensible planning and lead to other forms of waste. Would the changes make services more responsive to clients or would they distort the relationships between users and providers, distorting relationships based on trust with 'suspicious commercialism' (Le Grand and Bartlett, 1993, p 11)? And would the changes serve the interests of the poor and those in need rather than simply creating 'two-tier services that discriminate against and perhaps stigmatise, the most vulnerable people in our society' (Le Grand and Bartlett, 1993, p 11)? The answers, it was suggested, could depend on a number of factors, including: the market structure (whether there was genuine competition); the transaction costs; the level of information available – both to providers and to service users; and the motivations of both purchasers and providers, since it was argued that many of those working in welfare services were not 'commercially or financially motivated and find it difficult to make the shift from considering, say, the welfare of their users to the financial state of their provider unit' (Le Grand and Bartlett, 1993, p 31). These last two factors, particularly the information available to service users (including the information available about their rights and how to access these rights) and the motivations of those working in the public service sector, both emerge as major themes in the chapters that follow.

Meanwhile, as these questions continued to be debated, key elements of marketisation continued, although in differing forms, under New Labour governments (Esping Andersen et al, 2002; Finlayson, 2003; Whitfield, 2006; Powell, 2008). According to Whitfield, marketisation works by **commodifying** services and labour, increasing the scope for competition, creating opportunities for markets to develop and restructuring accountability mechanisms in public services (Whitfield, 2006). Central planning to meet social needs was to be replaced by planning via market forces, promoting competition among providers in the belief that they would respond to consumer preferences more appropriately and more cost-effectively. As has already been suggested, then, services were to be consumer led rather than producer led.

Whatever the rationale, critics have argued that the reality has been somewhat different. 'Marketisation is a long-term strategy', Whitfield opined, going on to argue that 'New Labour is dressing up choice as empowerment. But the real power in marketisation is gained by transnational companies and consultancies which provide services and, slowly but surely, take over the ownership of key public assets' (Whitfield, 2006, p 48). The implications for public sector employees, according to Whitfield, have included reductions in pay and conditions, including reductions in pensions. And they have included changes in organisation, management systems and structures as staff with private sector experience have been brought in to promote public service modernisation. Most importantly, service users – and would-be service users – have been faced with the increasing risks and inequalities that emanate from the market, with losers as well as winners as a result. As subsequent chapters demonstrate, there have been serious implications for Law Centres attempting to meet these increasing needs with tightening resources for the provision of legal aid, thereby reducing Law Centres' abilities to pursue test cases and campaigns in the wider public interest, as well as reducing their abilities to pursue cases for individual clients, more specifically.

Public service modernisation in practice

As Newman and Clarke (2009) and others have argued, public services have important roles to be considered, not simply in terms of delivering welfare but also in terms of their roles in enhancing citizenship and social cohesion – although they can also have a dark, controlling side. The New Public Management that was particularly prevalent in the context of neoliberalism, in the recent past, contained contradictions and ambiguities, leading to varying outcomes depending upon human agency and context. Like Whitfield, Newman and Clarke pointed to the ways in which the state had actually been creating markets either directly, through privatisation, or less directly through the construction of internal markets, the separation of purchasers and providers and through processes of competitive tendering. Significantly too, they concluded, market mechanisms were becoming embedded within public services more generally, suggesting that 'the binary distinction between state and market obscures the multiple ways in which markets, market-like mechanisms and market imagery have been deployed in reform programmes', with the increase of market discourse (Newman and Clarke, 2009, p 89).

While the 'New Managerialism' that accompanied these developments had been complex and internally inconsistent in some ways, typical features had included the following:

- 'attention to outputs and performance, rather than inputs;
- organizations being viewed as chains of low-trust relationships, linked by contracts or contractual type processes;
- the separation of purchaser and provider or client and contractor roles within formerly integrated processes or organizations;
- breaking down large scale organizations and using competition to enable "exit" or "choice" by service users;
- decentralization of budgetary and personal authority to managers' (Newman and Clarke, 2009).

As Newman (2009) pointed out in the same collection of essays, public service modernisation under New Labour governments differed from the New Right's New Public Management discourse in a number of ways – with its own internal inconsistencies and potential contradictions. It continued the attack on 'producer dominance', Newman argued, and it continued the aim of opening up more of the public sector to market mechanisms, just as it continued the emphasis on efficiency and performance and the search for business solutions to social and policy problems, in her judgement. But the discourse of public service modernisation under New Labour placed less emphasis on privatisation and competition per se, and greater emphasis on partnership working and democratic renewal. As Alan Milburn, MP (former cabinet minister and chief strategist of the election campaign for Labour's third term in office) expressed this, 'partnerships between the public and private sector are a cornerstone of the Government's modernisation programme in Britain. They are central to our drive to modernise key public services. Such partnerships are here and here to stay' (Milburn, 2001, p 33).

There was, in addition, despite the espoused interest in decentralisation and empowerment, greater emphasis on centrally imposed performance targets, 'exerting tighter controls over activities previously the province of professional judgement' (Newman, 2000, p 51). These latter aspects of modernisation emerge particularly strongly in later chapters in relation to Law Centres.

This notion of 'modernisation' has meant many different things, it has been argued (Flynn, 2007). It has been questioned whether the term has had any coherence, in fact (Finlayson, 2003). Powell, for example, identified six approaches, from modernisation as a means of improvement through to modernisation as the importation of private sector methods into the public sector and beyond (Powell, 2008). Newman and Clarke and their colleagues also highlighted such ambiguities, contradictions and internal tensions (Newman et al, 2008). It was important to understand these, they argued, in order to understand the scope for human agency as public service professionals and administrators addressed the challenges of these developing agendas.

As Barnes and Prior's collection of essays on *Subversive citizens* (Barnes and Prior, 2009) similarly argues, 'citizens are not "empty vessels" waiting to be filled with the attitudes and potentialities prescribed for them by dominant discourses', any more than professionals are, both practitioners and citizens being active agents with the capacity for counter-agency (Barnes and Prior, 2009, p 22). Further evidence has been emerging more recently still, demonstrating varying ways in which public service providers and others have been experiencing – and resisting – neoliberal marketisation strategies as these impacted upon them in practice (Hoggett et al, 2009; Manson, 2012; Murray, 2012). Later chapters similarly illustrate in more detail ways in which Law Centre staff and volunteers have been developing such counter strategies.

Professional ethos and values were indeed being challenged, and so were professionals' relationships with clients. As T.H. Marshall had earlier recognised, these relationships were rooted in professionals' ethical codes, based upon trust between professionals and their clients, while 'between buyer and seller there is not [that relationship of trust based upon professional codes of ethics]' (Marshall, 1950, p 133) – although he recognised that the professions 'have not always lived up to these high ideals' (Marshall, 1950, p 137), having also demonstrated the capacity for developing self-interested monopolies. The point, as Barnes and Prior also argued, was absolutely not to present some romantic view of professionals' counter-agency (Barnes and Prior, 2009). On the contrary, professionals, including lawyers, have provided ample illustration over the years of professional self-interest in practice, both in Britain and elsewhere, as the following chapter illustrates. Rather, the point was simply to identify the scope for contestation and oppositional consciousness both among professionals and among those who use their services, recognising the possibilities for alliances and shared strategies in the pursuit of common interests, including the pursuit of social justice agendas.

Subsequent chapters take up these themes, exploring the challenges to professional ethos and values and the strategies that have been developed in response.

TWO

Concepts of justice and access to justice

Before focusing upon the development of legal aid and the history of Law Centres, more specifically, this chapter starts by summarising different definitions and perspectives on social justice and their varying implications for social welfare. Among others, Piachaud has pointed to 'the very ambiguity of the term "social justice" – a "feel good" term that almost all can subscribe to' (Piachaud, 2008, p 33). While the pursuit of social justice 'has been the driving force behind much, perhaps most, social change', in Piachaud's view (Piachaud, 2008, p 50), 'opinions about what is fair and just have differed, and will probably always do so', he concludes.

Although similarities have been identified, there have also been significant differences of approach, both in theory and in practice. There has been widespread agreement about the importance of basic political liberties and fair process, together with widespread agreement about the importance of social rights, such as access to education, if citizens are to benefit from political rights, as Marshall argued (Marshall, 1950). But there has been far less agreement about what, if any, inequalities would be justifiable, and on what basis.

Rawls' *A theory of justice* (Rawls, 1971) has been centrally significant here as an influence on subsequent debates, sparking criticisms from varying perspectives. Deriving his arguments from processes of reasoning – as to what principles we would choose if we did not know what our own position and life chances were going to be – Rawls himself claimed that his conception of the principles of justice stood independently of any particular moral or religious views. He summarised the outcomes of these processes of reasoning as follows: 'All social primary goods – liberty and opportunity, income and wealth, and the social bases of self-respect – are to be distributed equally unless an unequal distribution of any, or all, of these goods is to the advantage of the least favoured' (Rawls, 1971, p 73). This was an argument not for defining justice in terms of absolute equality but, rather, that insofar as the outcomes were unequal, these inequalities could be justified according to Rawls' criteria. In his view, such an approach could form the basis for developing strategies for the promotion of justice across different types of societies. Or could it?

Rawls himself was focusing upon the rules for society as a whole, rather than upon the rules underpinning individual choices. Once the implications of his approach are unpacked and applied to individuals, however, Rawls' theory of social justice becomes more contentious from varying perspectives, as subsequent critics have argued. For example, Dworkin has argued that the outcomes could be unfair if the least-favoured were actually disadvantaged as a result of their own choices (Dworkin, 1981). As Wolff has pointed out, developing this type of argument, 'Some may be badly off because they are unable to work, or unable to find work. But others may have chosen to do no work. Can it be fair to tax the hardworking for the benefit of those who are capable of hard work, and equally talented, but choose to laze around instead?' (Wolff, 2008, p 19). This type of argument has been prevalent in recent debates on welfare reform and the issue of so-called scroungers under successive governments, illustrating some of the political differences underpinning debates on rights and justice in general, and welfare rights more specifically.

Others, including Sen (1992), have developed alternative responses to Rawls' approach, focusing instead upon the capabilities that people need in order to achieve effective functioning. While this capabilities approach implies the need for access to services such as education in order to develop these capabilities, Sen has himself refrained from spelling out the requirements in detail (although others such as Nussbaum (2003) have taken this further). This was because, in Sen's view, different societies need to engage in democratic ways of specifying what such functioning entails, in their own particular contexts. He pointed to the importance of taking account of both personal characteristics – sex, health/ability/disability and so on – and social aspects, including social norms and environmental factors. Unless these were taken into account, equalities of opportunity would fail to amount to equality in terms of overall freedoms, resulting in unjustifiable inequalities.

As Young, among others, has similarly pointed out, there has been a tendency for 'public and private institutions in contemporary liberal democratic societies to reproduce sexual, racial and class inequality by applying standards and rules in the same way to all who come under their purview' (Young, 2008, p 78), regardless of their unequal structural positions. 'Treating as equal those who are unequal does not produce equality' (Kennedy, 2005a, p 4). Equalisation for women in relation to the law has 'almost invariably been towards a male norm', is has been argued. (Kennedy, 2005a, p 3).

Justice, according to Fraser, requires a three-dimensional approach, then, taking account of:

- issues of redistribution (to address socio-economic inequalities)
- issues of recognition (challenging the hidden and not-so-hidden injuries of class, race and gender, such as social and cultural marginalisation and the lack of social respect) and
- issues of participation (challenging marginalisation and exclusion from political processes), including denial of 'the chance to press first-order justice claims in a given political community', the right to rights and the right to claim those rights (Fraser, 2008, p 280).

This last point has particular relevance for the issues addressed in this book, as will be argued in subsequent chapters. Each dimension has particular relevance too, in terms of race and ethnicity, as well as in terms of other forms of structural inequalities.

Without engaging in these debates in detail, the point to emphasise here is simply this: that the concept of justice, whether for individuals or societies, has been and continues to be contested, both within and between societies. As Sandel has opined more generally, the question is whether 'the principles of justice that govern the basic structure of society can be neutral in respect to the competing moral and religious convictions its citizens espouse' (Sandel, 1998, p 2). In his view, concepts of justice vary, depending, for example, upon whether societies place greater value on individual liberties and freedom of choice or whether they place greater emphasis on more collective, majoritarian approaches. Neither of these – liberal or communitarian – approaches represents satisfactory alternatives, in any case, according to Sandel, who concludes that 'rights depend for their justification on the moral importance of the ends they serve' (Sandel, 1998, p 3).

These ends have varied in different contexts over time. Previous approaches to social justice, as developed by such thinkers as R.H. Tawney, envisaged it in terms of promoting greater equality of outcomes (Bryson and Fisher, 2011). In contrast, more recent approaches have linked the promotion of social justice to economic goals (Bryson and Fisher, 2011). While the language of the Labour Party's Commission on Social Justice referred to the importance of the 'equal worth of all citizens' and the requirement 'that we reduce and where possible eliminate unjustifiable inequalities' (Commission on Social Justice, 1994, p 1), the report also emphasised that 'There will be no solid economic success without more social justice' (Commission on Social Justice, 1994, p 18). Far from 'being inimical to the neo-liberal values of economic efficiency, competitiveness and growth, social justice was actually a prerequisite for their effective realisation', according to Bryson and Fisher (2011, p 5) – a means towards economic goals rather than an end in itself. Bryson and Fisher criticised the 'decisive shift away from the idea that inequalities are an unjust product of class society and towards the New Labour idea that individuals should be given opportunities and responsibilities within such a society', with equal opportunities to compete for unequal outcomes – the view that was evidenced in the commission's report, they argued (Bryson and Fisher, 2011, p 5).

This touches on debates of central importance in relation to Law Centres, their aims, ethos and values, as will be suggested later. How far might social justice agendas be compatible with the operation of a market economy (Doyal and Gough, 1991; Burchardt and Craig, 2008)? Marxists have tended to critique rights-based approaches in such terms, going as far as to reject the possibility of achieving rights and justice within the context of capitalist societies, marked as they have been by inherent structural inequalities (Blackledge, 2012). As Blackledge, among others, has pointed out, Marx himself argued on occasion that workers' 'appeals to justice were pointless, since there are rival conceptions of justice formed by and informing the life of rival groups' (Blackledge, 2012, p 38) – in this case workers and their employers. Considerations of morality and justice were to be put aside in capitalist societies, it was argued, along with detailed consideration of what types of inequalities might be justifiable in socialist and communist societies. To address these issues in the here and now was to indulge in utopian fantasies.

While these types of argument have been influential within Marxist debates, others have challenged such dichotomous thinking. It was possible to engage with issues of rights and justice without abandoning a Marxist analysis of the underlying causes of inequality and social injustice. 'I think one can have one's cake and eat it – in this case at least', Callinicos has argued (Callinicos, 2001). By implication, then, rights for individual citizens could and should be pursued, but they needed to form a part of wider strategies for social change, addressing structural inequalities, taking account of the impacts of discrimination and oppression, past as well as present (including the legacies of slavery and racism, for example, as well as the legacies of discrimination in terms of gender, sexual orientation, age, religion and disabilities, to name some of the most obvious).

There is not the space here to explore these debates in further detail. The point to emphasise is simply this, that they have implications for Law Centres' distinctive aims, ethos and values, as will be argued later. Were Law Centres solely focused upon taking up individuals' cases, within the context of existing structural inequalities? Or were they also concerned to challenge such inequalities, taking test cases and campaigning as part of wider strategies to promote more broadly defined approaches to social justice? It was these wider strategies that were becoming particularly threatened, it will be suggested, which is not to underestimate the threats to their very survival too.

Public policies to promote access to justice

As the previous chapter has outlined, access to justice emerged as a central question in earlier debates on the establishment of the welfare state, illustrating the wider significance of these issues in the context of current debates on the future of welfare more widely. More specifically, the history of legal aid has been similarly linked (Sanderson and Sommerlad, 2011). As Geoffrey Bindman pointed out in an article explaining 'What made me a legal aid lawyer'): 'before the Second World War access to legal services by those who could not afford to pay for them was largely dependent on charity' (Bindman, 2002, p 512). While there was some provision for poor people to obtain representation in criminal cases, this was more limited in civil cases. Nor was there access to advice, except where this was given on a voluntary basis. **Pro bono** help was provided by what were known as 'poor men's lawyers' through legal aid societies. This was the situation that was to be addressed by the establishment of the Legal Aid Scheme in 1949. 'A new dawn was promised', Bindman (2002, p 515) explained, 'in which equality before the law would be made real by the elimination of personal wealth in determining access to legal advice and representation.' Access to justice was recognised as a fundamental right, then, in parallel with the rights to education, healthcare and social security, through the establishment of the welfare state.

Building upon the Beveridge Report's analysis, as the previous chapter explained, the post-war settlement was to tackle the causes of poverty and related social problems comprehensively through universal services, provided as rights, rather than on the basis of individualised charity. As already argued, T.H. Marshall's concept of citizenship included these social rights, alongside political rights and obligations (Marshall, 1950). As Marshall wrote, the civil element of citizenship was, in his view, 'composed of the rights necessary for individual freedom – liberty of the person, freedom of speech, thought and faith, the right to own property and to conclude valid contracts' and 'the right to justice'. And he continued: 'the last is of a different order from the others, because it is the right to defend and assert all one's rights on terms of equality with others and by due process of law' (Marshall, 1950, pp 10–11).

This point was emphasised by Sanderson and Sommerlad in their discussion of access to justice under New Labour governments. As they explain, not only are all other rights ultimately dependent on the right and ability to litigate on terms of equality with others, 'but the need of the disempowered for this right exceeds that of other citizens'. This was because, in their view, 'poor people are more likely to get into trouble with the law, come into contact with state agencies, suffer violence and abuse, experience precarious and sometimes dangerous employment, live in poor quality housing and be exploited by, for instance, private landlords' (Sanderson and Sommerlad, 2011, p 179). Civil justice problems were often linked to broader social, economic and health problems and power imbalances, they pointed out. Furthermore, 'the poor are more likely to feel powerless and not entitled to take action' (Sanderson and Sommerlad, 2011, p 180). Access to justice, then, was a key plank of the welfare state settlement, aiming, as the Beveridge Report did, to tackle the causes of poverty and related social ills.

In practice, though, the post-war settlement in relation to legal aid fell short of these aspirations, as did the rest of the welfare state more generally. By the mid-1960s, as the previous chapter explained, poverty was rediscovered as a persistent challenge, along with the limitations of other aspects of the welfare state. The limitations of legal aid in terms of the aspiration for equality of access to justice, regardless of the ability to pay, were similarly exposed (Abel-Smith, Zander and Brooke, 1973) – with housing and welfare problems as key areas of demand (reflecting, once again, the links with wider social inequalities).

This was the context in which the US's War on Poverty inspired interest in Britain, demonstrating alternative approaches to tackling these persistent challenges (Marris and Rein, 1967). The Office of Economic Opportunity (OEO), which emerged with this War on Poverty, established a Legal Services Program in 1965, hiring 2,000 full-time salaried lawyers in the first two years of its operations (reaching a total of some 6,000 by the late 1970s) and bringing legal representation to poor people in deprived neighbourhoods in many cities, towns, rural areas, migrant camps and Indian reservations (Johnson, 1999). While this represented a massive increase in access to legal services for individuals, the OEO's operations were by no means confined to this, however. Great emphasis was also placed upon pursuing collective approaches, taking class actions, taking up test cases and promoting legislative and administrative changes, in the interests of the poor.

In the early days these initiatives were, arguably, making a considerable impact. According to Kilwein (1999) legal services attorneys won important victories in the courts that reshaped the American welfare system, especially the programme that replaced the Aid to Dependent Children programme. 'Both conservative and liberal observers agree' that the Legal Services Program 'greatly increased the number of people receiving social welfare benefits' between 1967 and 1974, he argued (Kilwein, 1999, p 48), winning judicial decisions, in essence 'forcing the government to live up to its Great Society promises to the poor' (Kilwein, 1999, p 49). From the start this had been about an activist approach to the provision of legal services, aiming in the process to change the law for the benefit of the poor.

Whatever the underlying motives of the politicians who launched the War on Poverty (including their interests in reaching out to new potential voters for the Democratic Party, among Black Americans migrating from the deep South to the cities of the North), and whatever the underlying interests of the professional lawyers represented by the American Bar Association, the American welfare system was better funded for a period and 'the poor had a greater voice in its design' (Kilwein, 1999, p 45). The US approach to the provision of legal services to the poor was part of a broader programme of social reform, then, concerned with wider issues of social justice and social change.

Unsurprisingly, perhaps, given shifts in the political landscape, the Legal Services Program subsequently came under attack. This was not primarily as a result of attempts to contain expenditure, it has been argued (Johnson, 1999; Kilwein, 1999), although that was a factor too, even though the actual sums involved were relatively small in the context of overall budgets. More significantly, the programme came under attack because legal services lawyers were beginning to challenge vested interests, including major employers, landlords, insurance companies, bankers and the healthcare industry, not to forget the challenges to public institutions themselves. By the mid 1990s, when another Democratic president, Bill Clinton, was on the back foot, Kilwein argued, he signed legislation removing the right for publicly funded legal services to engage in policy issues affecting the poor and forbidding the pursuit of any new class action suits. Overall, these changes represented what has been described as 'a complete repudiation of the ideals of the legal services practice developed by the pioneers of the programme' (Kilwein, 1999, p 57), illustrating the contested nature of public policies to promote access to justice more generally.

But this is to leap forward to the future. In the late 1960s and early 1970s, the US Legal Services Program was seen as a potential model for addressing the shortcomings of legal aid in Britain – understandably, given the programme's impacts at that time, both in terms of providing services to individual clients and in terms of tackling the causes of poverty and injustice more widely.

The case for the provision of legal aid on the basis of the US model was described in the Society of Labour Lawyers' pamphlet *Justice for all*, published in 1968. This provided an outline of potential ways forward. Law Centres developed on such principles were to focus exclusively on the legal problems of poor people. In this way they could offer an alternative mode of service delivery, justifying the employment of salaried lawyers. This would be in contrast to the legal aid model of paying private practice lawyers on a case-by-case basis for such cases as they undertook for clients who were financially eligible under the scheme. In theory, this looked logical and attractive. If all the clients were eligible anyway, there was no point in the laborious process of sending individual approval applications to the legal aid authorities and submitting invoices for the work done for each client.

In the event, however, the government of the day was not interested in setting up a network of such centres in Britain and it was left to more local initiatives. In 1970 the first Law Centre was set up in North Kensington, London, soon to be followed by Law Centres in Paddington, Islington and Camden, resourced with local authority and other sources of funding. Although the Law Society was initially doubtful or even hostile, by the end of the 1970s (with support from the then Lord Chancellor) an accommodation had been reached and the Society came round to the view that, far from being a threat, Law Centres were actually generating additional work for private practice (Smith, 1997). The total number of Law Centres rose to 62, at their peak (with funding from a range of sources, including inner-city regeneration initiatives, as well as some funding from central government for a limited number of centres).

Like their counterparts in the US, Australia and Canada (Zemans and Thomas, 1999), these Law Centres aimed to close the gap between the law and individuals and communities, especially individuals and communities in deprived areas, taking up test cases with wider implications and undertaking public legal education, as well as providing information and advice to individual clients. They were to provide specialist legal advice and representation in social welfare law, including welfare rights, disability rights, immigration and asylum, housing and homelessness, employment, community care and all forms of discrimination including racial discrimination. While these areas of law were the ones most commonly provided, a smaller number of Law Centres also offered advice in mental health, education rights and young people and children's rights, depending on the local need for these particular services.[1]

At this point it should be emphasised that Law Centres developed their remits in response to local needs, as these emerged, adding areas of provision when required – and dropping others, such as juvenile crime and personal injury, when demands for these were being met elsewhere. There were issues of prioritisation to be addressed here. In the early days Law Centres developed their remits in the context of increasing opportunities for promoting rights as social welfare law and equalities legislation developed in the 1970s and 1980s. These changes opened up new opportunities, potentially increasing public awareness of the possibilities for taking up and pursuing rights through legal processes.

Legal services had not previously been made available to the public outside the for-profit structure of private practice firms, and lawyers had had only that structure within which to pursue their careers. Law Centres also offered new vocational opportunities, typically organised on a collective basis, reflecting their commitment to democratic, participative values and ways of working, with democratic accountability to the communities that they were there to serve. In the early days of relative independence for community Law Centres they were closely linked, in many instances, to local community organisations and social movements, actively engaged in community work. Subsequent chapters consider these aspects in more detail.

These early days were succeeded by more challenging times, however. Funding had always been relatively precarious, with low levels of local government funding and minimal direct central government funding. So, as funding from these sources began to dry up, Law Centres started to operate the legal aid scheme, submitting applications in behalf of eligible clients and invoicing for the work, thus guaranteeing themselves a source of funding from the statutory scheme. But the costs of legal aid were growing, overall, and this became a matter of political concern as part of wider pressures to contain public expenditure more generally.

Although the growth in legal aid expenditure was actually far more pronounced in respect of private firms than it was for Law Centres (which were facing increasing competition from advice agencies as well as from the private sector), by the 1990s a considerable proportion of their income was coming from legal aid casework. Even before the Carter reforms, Law Centres faced major challenges, then, as governments focused upon devising ways of managing costs and obtaining efficiency savings, including via competitive contracting processes. By this time a number of private practice firms had discovered that a reasonable living could be made by concentrating almost exclusively on legal aid work – a far cry from the situation in the 1970s, when legal aid had constituted a tiny proportion of the work of most more broadly based practices. To government, there was no logical distinction to be drawn, then, between these legal aid firms and legal aid-dependent Law Centres.

The Carter proposals for reform

Having failed to contain costs effectively (particularly the costs of criminal legal aid, rather than the costs of civil legal aid, incidentally) the New Labour government commissioned Lord Carter to come up with proposals to gain more control over these costs. In the event, it was the proposals that impacted on civil legal aid that became the focus for reform, rather than the more costly criminal legal aid costs.

The Carter Report of 2006 critiqued the way in which legal aid work was being administered and contracted and suggested that there was 'scope for greater efficiency in the way that not for profit organisations deliver legal advice services' (Lord Carter of Coles, 2006, p 45). The previous model of funding, the report continued, may encourage inefficiency, as by paying for hours worked rather than cases completed it may encourage some caseworkers to spend more time on cases than is strictly necessary. This could mean fewer clients helped, and in an environment where ever more innovative means are being found to help more people access legal advice, it is essential that a good quality service is secured that provides maximum value for money. (Lord Carter of Coles, 2006, p 45)

This report, which was endorsed by the Legal Services Commission (LSC), was followed by the introduction of the **Unified Contract** in 2007 – a new system by which Law Centres and other legal aid providers were to be contracted and paid. These contracts were to be awarded on the basis of competitive tendering processes for bulk contracts.

With the introduction of the Unified Contract, payment was no longer based on the hours that were actually worked for particular cases but on fixed fees for different types of cases, calculated by the LSC itself. Specifically, the fixed fee scheme meant that the providers of legal advice, such as Law Centres, were being paid between £160 and £250 per case, depending on the area of law (for example employment, debt, welfare benefit and housing). There was provision for 'exceptional' cases to be paid at higher rates, but this applied only to cases that consumed more than three times the amount of time allowed for the regular fixed fee cases. As subsequent sections argue in more detail, this fixed fee system was very controversial, critics arguing that most of the Law Centres' cases fell between these two levels, requiring more time than the regular fixed fee allowed but falling short of the requirements for payment at the higher 'exceptional' level .

Legal aid reforms 2007, following the Carter report in 2006

The Carter reforms – a 'market-based approach to reform' – have been described as exemplifying New Labour's attempt to 'reconcile a discourse of social justice with the techniques of New Public Management and the parallel discourse of commitment to the citizen as a public consumer' (Sanderson and Sommerlad, 2011, p 178), 'nuanced to the point of self-contradiction' (Sanderson and Sommerlad, 2011, p 183). In Baroness Helena Kennedy's view, 'the so called reforms to legal aid served only to significantly weaken it' (Kennedy, 2009, p vi).

In summary, government efforts to contain costs were to focus upon increasing marketisation (through the competitive tendering process), coupled with what has been described as the micro-management of legal aid transactions through the administrative systems required by the **commissioning** agent, the LSC. Advice was being measured in terms of what might be readily measurable – the volumes of advice units provided – rather than in terms of impact on the lives of individuals in disadvantaged communities or the contribution of legal aid to the promotion of access to justice more generally. The implications, it has been argued, were that 'poor people's problems could be worth only two or three hours of a paralegal's time, and no more', reducing legal aid to a '*sink service* for people on means-tested benefits' (Sanderson and Sommerlad, 2011, p 194). This, Sanderson and Sommerlad concluded, corresponded to Crouch's characterisation of neoliberal reforms as involving the residualisation, distortion and degradation of public sector services more generally (Crouch, 2011).

As subsequent chapters argue, there were potential challenges here for Law Centres, which, despite this increasingly challenging neoliberal climate, were aiming to preserve their varied but distinctive contributions to the goal of access to justice for all, regardless of the ability to pay. These distinctive contributions have been summarised (Smith, 1997) as including the following:

- reaching minority communities (and opening up access to legal careers to wider constituents in the process)
- supporting effective campaigning for social justice,
- taking up issues of collective concern in communities
- pursuing test cases to challenge discrimination and
- promoting public legal education and preventative approaches more widely.

These were the types of distinctive contributions that had characterised the provision of legal services as part of the US War on Poverty, rooted in wider strategies for social change and increasing social justice in the US and elsewhere (Regan et al, 1999). But none of these distinctive contributions was fundable under the Carter reforms, which focused solely upon the funding of units of advice and directly related case-work activities. The reforms were based upon a relatively narrow conception of access to justice, focusing upon individuals' concerns rather than on taking a more collective approach to addressing the underlying causes of poor people's legal problems as part of wider strategies for social justice.

Potential issues for legal professionals

As Burdett's study of Law Centres (Burdett, 2004) demonstrated, challenges of funding and administration could be located within broader challenges to the welfare state. As Chapter One has already argued, these policy shifts were part of wider agendas to increase efficiency and enhance consumer choice – using market mechanisms to control the behaviours of public sector employees and public service professionals. 'Everyone who works in the public sector, lives in the same household as a public-sector worker, or who has children of school age, lives in the shadow of the anxious, inspectorial culture that promises to visit the shame of failure upon us … Governments have not wished to trust professionals, and thus they have opted to control them', it has been argued (Cooper, 2008, p 39, quoted in Bryson and Deery, 2011, p 107).

The point is absolutely not to suggest that professionals in general, or Law Centre staff more specifically, should not be publicly accountable. As Paterson and Sherr, among others, have argued, quality, value for money and efficient management are rarely off the agenda (Paterson and Sherr, 1999) – nor should they be. Rather, the question is whether the increasing use of market mechanisms represents the most appropriate or even the most effective way of ensuring the achievement of these goals. Were they even counter-productive?

Burdett's study of Law Centres questioned whether they might be. Were the next generations of staff and volunteers being formed in such a different context that the public service ethos was at risk of being undermined? Was motivation increasingly pragmatic and individualistic? Were volunteers more concerned with developing their CVs, for instance, rather than with focusing upon campaigning for access to justice for all? These concerns formed part of wider processes of questioning about neoliberalism's long-term impacts, including its impacts upon professionalism and professional values.

Was the neoliberal emphasis upon individual choice empowering service users and driving public service modernisation, as successive governments claimed it was? Or was the very notion of 'public value', together with the public service ethos itself, being undermined by these processes of marketisation and posing new challenges for those concerned with professional ethics and values (Banks, 2004; Hoggett et al, 2009; Benington and Moore, 2010)? The following chapter explores in more detail the contested notions of professionalism and the public service ethos in the context of increasing marketisation. This sets the framework for discussing the dilemmas that were being posed for Law Centre staff and volunteers, in subsequent chapters. How were these dilemmas being addressed and, in terms of the emotional labour involved, at what costs?

Before we move on to these debates, the potential implications of the proposed reforms – and professional reactions to them – need to be summarised more specifically, so as to set the context more precisely. The Law Society had already expressed concerns about the Carter proposals before they were implemented, arguing that the fixed fee system would reduce the supply of lawyers prepared to undertake legal aid work, encourage cherry-picking (that is, taking on only the cases that could be resolved most easily within the scheme's time allocations) and impact most seriously on the most vulnerable clients (Law Society, 2006). Private lawyers also submitted critical responses to the LSC consultation, as the following extract demonstrates, arguing that 'the scheme you propose will prejudice vulnerable and disabled clients, especially those with mental difficulties, most of whom we represent, as their cases take longer to prepare…. [It] will also discriminate against clients from minority ethnic groups where language barriers often mean it takes twice as long to prepare and advise on their cases' (quoted in Sanderson and Sommerlad, 2011, p 188).

It could, of course, be argued that 'they would say that, wouldn't they?', since lawyers (sometimes described in the mass media as 'fat cat lawyers' profiting from legal aid) stood to lose out financially from the fixed fee system.

Abel's study of the legal profession in England and its responses to pressures for increasing marketisation (Abel, 2003) provides detailed evidence illustrating both sides of the argument. Lawyers understandably resented the ways in which they were being portrayed by politicians. Debates on proposals for reform, back in the Thatcher years, had presented them as suspect and 'shameless' (Abel, 2003, p 86), committed to restrictive practices in order to further their own professional interests, rather than to safeguarding their clients' best interests. This was part of wider attacks on professions at that time for what Abel described as a mixture of motives, ideological attacks based on the view of professional organisations such as the Bar Council and the Law Society as forms of trade unions (that is, promoting restrictive practices), plus concerns with cost control and populism. Abel wrote that 'some voters disliked lawyers even more than Thatcher' (Abel, 2003, p xiii).

The election of the New Labour government in 1997 might have seemed to promise greater commitment to legal aid (although no new money was actually promised). But attempts to eliminate restrictive practices were still firmly on the agenda. Even before its election, New Labour had produced a justice policy that included references to the need to reduce the scope for what was described as the wide abuse of legal aid by 'unreasonable litigants and greedy lawyers' (Abel, 2003, p 273), and accusations that lawyers were seeking to protect their vested interests. This was the background to New Labour's attempts to apply public service modernisation strategies to the legal professions.

But was there any justification for these types of criticism? Was professional self-regulation actually working in the best interests of clients and in the best interests of society at large? By 1998 there was recognition that all was not well within the professions themselves, with the *New Law Journal* predicting the end of self-regulation (Abel, 2003, p 405). The battle against legal aid cuts could have been won, it was argued, if the Law Society had set itself to root out restrictive practices earlier. While for some the problem was that there had not been sufficiently vigorous opposition to the government's proposals, for others the problem was also the profession's failure to set its own house in order. There were, in addition, criticisms of past failures to address sexism and institutional racism in the professions, pointing to the under-representation of women in the Law Society's Council, as judges or as partners in law firms, for example. It was argued that these institutional biases impacted on women and black and ethnic minorities before the courts, where myths and stereotypes were disfiguring the legal process (Kennedy, 2005a).

While critics such as Kennedy pointed to the importance of addressing these issues, this was absolutely not such as to endorse caricatures of all lawyers as 'greedy fat cats'. On the contrary, there were significant differences *within* the profession in terms of the rewards to be reaped – and who was reaping them. For instance, while 50% of law students were female by the beginning of the 21st century, the majority, Kennedy argued, were being 'steered towards public service law, by which I mean fields largely funded out of legal aid'. 'The men make career choices much more related to money and prestige and head for high-rewarding areas of practice', she continued, but far from embarking upon careers as potential 'fat cats', 'women find their place doing poor folks' law', the least rewarded areas of legal practice (Kennedy, 2005a, p 2).

There is not the space to go into these debates in any detail. The point is simply to emphasise the importance of taking criticisms of the professions seriously and focusing upon ways of ensuring their accountability – while discounting the populist rhetoric of some of their opponents. These criticisms potentially applied to professionals such as lawyers. But lawyers were also concerned with challenging the decisions of officials and, indeed, the decisions of professionals providing other services too. Who, then, was guarding the guardians? Once again, the question was not whether but how accountability mechanisms could be most effectively ensured – via the increasing use of market mechanisms or via strengthened forms of democratic accountability, including accountability to service users and their surrounding communities?

For Law Centres, the Carter proposals posed these challenges in very particular ways, as subsequent chapters explore in more detail.

Before we move on to these, however, two other elements of the proposed changes needs to be considered in summary: the attempt to bring legal services together to develop more joined-up approaches and more recent legislation reducing the scope of legal aid more generally.

Community Legal Advice Centres and Community Legal Advice Networks

While the Carter reforms of 2007 have undoubtedly had far-reaching effects on Law Centres, there have been other changes too, impacting on the ways in which Law Centres have been operating. Even before the implementation of the Carter reforms, after the publication of the consultation paper *Making legal rights a reality* in 2005, the LSC had set out to pilot a scheme that aimed to develop partnerships among legal service providers. This scheme sought to build Community Legal Advice Centres (CLACs) in urban areas and Community Legal Advice Networks (CLANs) in rural areas in order to offer legal advice in more integrated and cost-effective ways. The LSC's objective was that this 'joined-up approach' (LSC, 2005) would be 'run through a lead supplier' who would then act as an interface with the LSC. This, so the consultation paper argued, 'would reduce transaction costs on all sides and would allow the delegation of some LSC functions to the lead supplier' (LSC, 2005, p 41).

Although the idea of collaborative working and creating partnerships had widely been positively received, there were concerns about the ways in which the CLACs and CLANs were to be implemented (Hansen, 2006). A response from the Advice Services Alliance[2] (ASA, 2005) to the LSC's 2005 consultation paper critiqued the plans of the LSC for being inadequately researched and for lacking details on implementation and costs. The ASA further questioned the LSC's proposal as not including immigration and asylum law within social welfare law.

The main concern put forward by the ASA, however, was that the top-down approach to the implementation of CLACs failed to take into appropriate consideration the strong community links and local knowledge of existing providers. There were fears that many advice agencies might 'go up the wall or survive in subsistence form', as Hynes and Robins put it, if they were not included in the CLAC or CLAN (Hynes and Robins, 2009, p 76). In short, while there were already ambitions to develop joined-up approaches to the provision of legal advice, there were also major concerns. In the view of Hynes and Robins, for example: 'The CLAC initiative combines the best and worst of recent policy thinking on legal aid. The central idea to have better local planning of services is right but the project appears to be compromised by a crude and divisive tendering process with little respect for the providers' (Hynes and Robins, 2009, p 75). Chapter Six considers in more detail the issues involved in attempts to promote collaboration in the face of increasing pressures for competition.

More recent legislative changes

The proposals for the introduction of CLACs and CLANs posed potential challenges, then, in addition to the Law Centres' earlier concerns about the implementation of the Carter reforms more generally. More recently, the policy context has again shifted significantly, as the Coalition government has developed its own proposals for further reform. In particular, the Legal Aid, Sentencing and Punishment of Offenders Bill (LASPO) (passed as an Act in 2012) had potentially major implications for Law Centres' future funding and viability, especially for those most reliant on legal aid funding. This was because the legislation set out to reduce the scope of legal aid as well as to change the eligibility criteria and the fee structure. In total, the Ministry of Justice expected to make savings of up to £350 million on the legal aid budget, which then amounted to a little above £2 billion (Ministry of Justice, 2010, p 5).[3] The most significant savings in the legal aid budget, as Cookson suggested, would be made 'by changing the scope of Legal Aid by removing many cases from coverage' (Cookson, 2011, p 72), accounting for an estimated £280 million (gross) or around 80% of the savings. While criminal legal aid would (for the time being at least) remain available for those who 'cannot afford to pay for their own representation', civil legal aid was expected to be reduced considerably. In general, most areas of social welfare law were planned to be taken out of the scope of legal aid unless they were explicitly included as staying within scope. Specifically, the government planned to remove legal aid from employment advice (except in discrimination cases), from debt advice (except when someone's home was at immediate risk), from welfare benefits advice, from immigration law (except in cases of detention), from divorce law and from school exclusion appeals as well as from clinical negligence and personal injury cases. The areas for which legal aid was expected to receive continued funding included family law cases that involved domestic violence and forced marriage or child abduction (Ministry of Justice, 2010). Apart from these changes in the scope of legal aid, the government also proposed to introduce a means-tested contribution in legal aid cases, resulting in those with assets of more than £1,000 having to pay at least £100 of their legal costs.[4]

As a result of these proposed changes to legal aid, it was estimated that '605,000 people might be affected, of whom an estimated 595,000 might no longer receive Legal Aid as a result of removing specified law categories from scope and around 10,000 might now pay contributions or be subject to higher contributions' (Ministry of Justice, 2011a, p 11). More recent figures have estimated an even higher number of 623,000 people losing out on advice on civil legal problems as a result of the reductions in the scope of legal aid (Hynes, 2012). Independent research (Cookson, 2011) suggested, however, that a reduction in legal aid spending in areas such as social welfare and family law as well as clinical negligence (£240 million, or 85% of the £280 million saving) might create considerable knock-on costs of £139 million, which might amount to 42% of the predicted savings, calling into question the government's estimated savings from the legal aid budget.

While recent changes in the scope of legal aid had not fully crystallised at the time of this writing, in terms of their long-term consequences for Law Centres the effects of the Carter reforms, implemented in 2007, have become apparent. The following chapters (Chapter Three and Chapter Four) explore the challenges posed by these changes and the consequent dilemmas experienced by Law Centre workers and volunteers. Later chapters then go on to explore specific themes in further detail, including the views of other **stakeholders** in the face of increasing challenges for the longer term.

Notes

[1] www.lawcentres.org.uk/lawcentres/detail/what-do-law-centres-do/ (last accessed 1 March 2012).

[2] An umbrella organisation for independent advice networks in the UK consisting of 2,000 providers of advice, including Law Centres and Citizens Advice Bureaux (CAB).

[3] See also news.bbc.co.uk/democracylive/hi/house_of_commons/newsid_9674000/9674331.stm (last accessed 4 March 2012). The legal aid budget of £2.146 billion for the year 2009/2010 was comprised of £1.205 billion for criminal legal aid and £0.941 billion for civil legal aid (Ministry of Justice, 2011a, p 9).

[4] www.bbc.co.uk/news/uk-11741289 (last accessed 4 March 2012).

[5] www.justice.gov.uk/legal-aid/newslatest-updates/legal-aid-reform

THREE

Ethos and values

This chapter starts by summarising competing perspectives on the public service ethos and professional ethics more specifically, building on the discussion of competing perspectives on lawyers in the preceding chapter. Considerable claims have been made about professional altruism; claims which have in turn been subjected to fundamental challenges. Public service professionals have been faced with increasing dilemmas, in the context of public service modernisation, in attempting to balance competing demands despite the pressures to reduce the space for the exercise of professional judgement. This introductory section sets the context for the later focus on Law Centres and those who were working in them, starting with their motivations and values as these interrelate with Law Centres' own missions and ethos. Subsequent sections explore the reflections of those directly involved with Law Centres, and reflections by stakeholders from different sectors: lawyers in private practice, staff from other voluntary sector agencies such as advice centres, local authority officers and councillors and funders more generally.

Contested approaches to the public service ethos, professional ethics and professionalism in the context of public service modernisation

Differing approaches to the contested notion of the public service ethos need to be unpacked so as to set the context for the discussion of ethics and the professions. Is there a public service ethos, and, if so, how might it be changing in response to public service modernisation? In summary, the public service ethos was traditionally associated with notions of service to the public within the framework of public institutions such as the civil service, and characterised by commitments to values such as those of accountability and impartiality, delivering services according to agreed procedures, doing a socially useful job without fear or favour.

The question of motivation has been involved here, the public service motivation construct being defined as an individual's predisposition to respond to motives associated with public institutions (Perry and Wise, 1990) and to behave accordingly. Altruism – the commitment to serving the public, even if this might involve lower rates of pay in public service employment – has been defined as a central aspect of this motivation, although more rationally self-interested motives such as job security have also been identified as potentially relevant, in the past at least (Perry and Honeghem, 2008). Individuals can and do act with varying motivations.

Social democratic approaches to the welfare state have tended to place particular emphasis upon notions of reciprocity, mutuality and solidarity. As Chapter One has already suggested, Titmuss, for example, explored altruism in terms of acting 'reciprocally, giving and receiving service for the well-being of the whole community' (Titmuss, 1970, p 213), recognising the common benefits of public services universally available on the basis of need, rather than on the basis of ability to pay for them. This latter approach seemed to have particular relevance for Law Centre staff and volunteers, as later chapters illustrate.

More recently, the notion of the public service ethos has become more controversial, as critics have emphasised associations with bureaucratic dysfunctionality and paternalism (Le Grand, 2003). It was suggested that public officials were using this notion as a smoke-screen and providing spurious justifications for bureaucratic inefficiencies and inertia. The logic of agendas for public service modernisation was to question the continuing relevance of the public service ethos, given that public services were being increasingly delivered in other ways, driven by market-led forms of accountability to service users. As the House of Commons Public Administration Select Committee's report on *The public service ethos* argued, the public service ethos was not different from or superior to that of the private or voluntary sector (House of Commons, 2002). Public servants (including MPs, of course) could behave in corrupt and unethical ways, just as individuals in the private sector could deliver services according to the highest ethical standards.

While recognising that individuals may indeed be motivated by, and may or not behave in ways that resonate with, the characteristics of the public service ethos, this still leaves the question as to whether there may be differences between *sectors*. Is their primary goal to provide services to the public or to make profits for their shareholders and partners? This issue emerges later in the context of Law Centres and their experiences and relationships with private sector law firms.

The Public Administration Select Committee's report went on to suggest a public service code, starting from the principles of probity, transparency and accountability that were supposed to underpin public life overall. Public servants should also focus upon providing quality services, treating public service workers and their clients fairly and equitably. There should be proper redress where maladministration had occurred (a central concern for Law Centres, of course). And public service providers should remember at all times that 'public service means serving the public, not serving the interests of those who provide the service, and work collaboratively with others to this end' (House of Commons, 2002, p 6) – a comment reflecting the distrust of public servants and professionals that underpinned public service modernisation agendas in the first place.

Was the public service ethos being undermined, then, as a result of this distrust, which was accompanied by the increasing use of marketised incentives such as performance-related pay? John and Johnson (2008) examined the evidence for this argument and concluded that it was not borne out by the data. Despite anxieties about the impact of public service modernisation, there were still differences between employees in the public sector and those in the private sector in terms of the sources of job satisfaction, for example (with greater emphasis being placed upon whether the job was useful to society, allowing opportunities to help other people, for instance). John and Johnson also found that younger people seemed to demonstrate as much commitment to public service values as did older employees, although they were tentative in offering possible explanations for the apparently relatively high levels of commitment among the young. There seemed to be evidence that the public service ethos still existed among both older workers and their younger colleagues. But this in no way implied that they would be immune from demotivation in response to future changes.

In summary, the notion of the public service ethos has been highly controversial, raising questions that underpin debates on the professions and on professional motivations and ethics in the context of public service modernisation. These issues, including the generational issues involved, emerge later in relation to the values of Law Centres and their staff and volunteers.

Ethics and the professions

Ethics and the related notion of 'ethos' have been centrally important yet similarly contentious topics in debates on the professions, professionalism and the future of public welfare provision more generally. On the one hand, professionals have been presented (or at least, have presented themselves) as 'knights in shining armour' (Le Grand, 2003). The most frequently cited traits that have been described as characterising professionals have been their membership of an organisation that promulgates 'standards and/or ideals of behaviour' and that 'they publicly pledge themselves to render assistance to those in need and as a consequence have special responsibilities or duties not incumbent upon others who have not made this pledge' to use their specialist knowledge and skills in such altruistic ways (Banks, 2004, p 19). In summary, professionals should be motivated not solely by the cash nexus, without regard to the relevant professional standards. Obvious examples include the commitment that lawyers should not obstruct the course of justice by continuing to pursue a case if a wealthy corporate client were to admit their guilt to their lawyer while continuing to protest their innocence in court.

Conversely, professionals have been presented as 'knaves', motivated by their own self-interest, operating restrictive practices for the benefit of service providers, rather than working in the best interests of service users. According to those holding more sceptical views, 'professionals surround their work with an ideological covering. It is a "calling", not merely a job', professionals claim, 'carried out from high motives of altruism, of glory, or of moral, spiritual or aesthetic commitment, rather than for mundane gain' (Collins, 1990). But these types of claims can be seen as rhetorical devices, it has been argued in response, justifying the use of professional power and privilege (Wilding, 1982). As Chapter One has already suggested, there was evidence of such potentially negative views of public service professionals from the post-war period onwards (and, indeed, before that too); negative views that were compounded by feminists and anti-racists, who were deeply critical of the paternalism and institutional racism that in their view was too often displayed (Williams, 1989).

In recent times, more general criticisms have been associated with the managerialism that was so prevalent from the late 1970s. As Page, for example, has argued, New Labour was 'skeptical of the claim that welfare professionals, motivated by a public service ethic, can be relied upon to develop high quality, cost efficient services without external monitoring' (Page, 2007, p 109). Targets, performance monitoring and audits were required in order to control their potential for exhibiting more knavish behaviours in practice, as the previous chapter has suggested in relation to lawyers engaged in legal aid work more specifically. Critics such as Standing have argued more generally that increased monitoring of professionals illustrated society's lack of trust in professionals to be professional (Standing, 2011), setting the UK's New Labour government's approach in the context of similar strategies being developed internationally.

The points to emphasise here are simply as follows. The issue of professional ethics has been contested from varying perspectives. As with debates on ethics more generally, there have been competing approaches, based on differing theoretical underpinnings, as to what might and what might not constitute ethical behaviours. This suggests that professionals have needed and continue to need the space to exercise their judgement, weighing up competing claims. Public service provision has been conceptualised as having been particularly challenging in these respects, a dilemmatic space in which there may be no self-evidently right thing to do (Honig, 1996). Both professionals and street-level bureaucrats have experienced tensions, it has been argued, in attempting to balance colliding value systems and competing demands in the public sphere (Lipsky, 1980; Hoggett et al, 2009). These pressures have become increasingly problematic in the context of public service modernisation.

Differing approaches and outcomes

Before we move on to consider the implications for Law Centres, these differing approaches need some brief introduction, together with the range of potential outcomes in terms of professional motivations and behaviours. In summary, approaches based upon Kantian principles have stressed the importance of absolute values as rules for guidance, such as the categorical imperative of commitment to the best interests of each individual client. For example, the doctor's first duty, according to a Kantian approach, would be to each individual patient, recommending treatment according to the best interests of that particular individual. Rationing access to expensive medication or treatments would have no place here, in terms of the professional ethics involved. Although doctors have been understandably reluctant to become directly involved in rationing decisions within the context of the NHS, the reality has been more complex. In practice, like other professionals, doctors have actually made and continue to make decisions with rationing implications, such as decisions about how to allocate their time so as to meet varying needs most effectively. In periods of austerity the pressures to make judgements about the allocation of scarce resources have been increasing across a range of professions, including the legal profession, as has already been suggested.

Approaches based upon utilitarian principles, in contrast, start from the principle of the greatest good of the greatest number of people, implying that professionals need to balance the interests of individual clients and communities with the interests of society more widely. But who decides what would be in the best interests of the majority, and on what basis? And how would such approaches impact upon the rights of minorities, especially disadvantaged minorities? Arguments of the utilitarian kind have been used to justify – or to challenge – limits to the time that lawyers can spend with any particular legal aid client, in order to ensure that as many clients as possible receive some form of service, however time restricted, as the previous chapter has demonstrated. But the legal profession has questioned whether such forms of rationing would meet the needs of the most disadvantaged clients.

These underlying differences of approach have had varying implications for professional ethics, and especially for professionals providing public services in periods of public expenditure constraint. As Banks and others have pointed out (Banks, 2004; Hugman, 2005), professional codes of ethics have varied from country to country in any case, as well as from profession to profession, over time. This is not to suggest that any one ethical code is the moral equivalent of another. Rather, the point to emphasise is that ethical codes are varied and contested. While codes may provide guidance, this is not to the exclusion of the need for professional judgement.

In the current context however, as Banks (2004) has also noted, ethical codes have tended to become more prescriptive. And as codes become longer and more prescriptive, the room for trust and discretion gets narrower. This tendency, it has been argued, has been an increasingly marked effect in response to new modes of management in the public services. Although there have been some differences of view as to the extent to which professional discretion has been curtailed in practice (Clarke and Newman, 1997; Evans, 2010), the trend has been well marked. In the 1990s, for instance, Hoggett described the combined effects of successive government attempts to get 'more for less' in terms of new and more sophisticated forms of organisational control (Hoggett, 1996) – challenging professional self-regulation, as the previous chapter has illustrated in relation to the legal profession. In Hoggett's view, control mechanisms were increasingly centralised, despite the simultaneous promotion of strategies claiming to promote decentralisation and self-regulation within the public services. Some senior professionals had become professional-managers as a result, while 'the diffusion of management systems has clearly had the effect of reducing professional autonomy across a wide number of sectors' (Hoggett, 1996, pp 28–9), potentially undermining motivation and trust in the process (Hoggett, 1996; Hoggett et al, 2009; Sommerlad, 2001).

This leads into the next point to be noted in relation to this study: the increasing interest in 'virtue ethics' in response to some of the challenges of the new managerialism (Banks and Gallagher, 2009). A virtue ethics framework, it has been argued, 'can provide an orientation to professional attitudes and actions that offers a welcome counter-weight to the current emphasis on obligation-based performance to externally defined principles, rules and standards' (Banks and Gallagher, 2009, p 49). Here the focus shifts away from targets and outputs to emphasise, in contrast, the 'virtues' required of the professional in question; virtues such as professional wisdom, care, respectfulness, trustworthiness, justice, courage and integrity. The individual professional is defined as a moral agent within a community of practitioners who share a core moral purpose or service ideal (Banks and Gallagher, 2009).

Virtue ethics has its critics too. This type of approach is not unproblematic, and does not provide unproblematic answers for professional practice within the context of public service modernisation. Ethical issues and dilemmas are, arguably, inherent in the exercise of professional judgement per se (Hoggett et al, 2009). The point for the purposes of this study is simply to emphasise the tensions that virtue ethics highlight, and the potential conflicts for professionals in the current policy context.

The outcomes, meanwhile, continue to emerge. What Banks describes as the 'new accountability' upwards has been associated with processes of de-professionalisation, restricting the space for professional discretion and potentially threatening professional ethics more generally (Banks, 2004). But this is not the only view, or indeed the only possible outcome. For some professionals, for example, the new professionalism could be positively associated with more effective uses of scarce resources and/or more responsive outcomes for service users, to be welcomed as such. For others, more pragmatically, these challenges needed to be met by more professional entrepreneurialism, as the only realistic basis for survival in an increasingly competitive climate.

Alternatively, professionals may respond to what they perceive as threats to their professional integrity with reluctant conformity or by developing individual or collective forms of non-compliance (Banks, 2004; Hoggett et al, 2009; Sommerlad, 2010). Sommerlad's earlier study of legal aid lawyers quotes Downs (1966) in this context: 'the greater the efforts made to control subordinated officials, the greater the efforts by those subordinates to evade or counteract such "control"' (Downs, 1966). The effects of such control strategies may actually be perverse, encouraging knavish rather than knightly behaviours in order to achieve the required targets. As Sommerlad added, by way of illustration, a lawyer commented that '"I have to go into the office this weekend and forge a whole lot of stuff for the audit. That's what I really hate; I think I was a good lawyer, maybe not perfect, but I was certainly never dishonest; and that's what this is making me"' (Sommerlad, 2001, p 355).

Finally, professionals may respond with what Banks has described as 'principled quitting', 'jumping ship' in order to retain personal integrity when all other strategies seem to have failed (Banks, 2004). Later chapters provide illustrations of each of these types of response to the ethical issues and dilemmas posed by public service modernisation and more recent policy developments in relation to the provision of legal aid.

Law Centres, their missions and ethos

How were these potential dilemmas being experienced in Law Centres? What were Law Centres themselves setting out to do and in what ways did the services that they were offering differ from those being offered by other providers? How were those involved, whether as staff or as volunteers, describing Law Centres? And how were Law Centres being perceived by other stakeholders, including lawyers in private practice, as well as people working in CABs and other advice agencies, or by local authorities and other funders?

Law Centres' ethos emerged as intertwined with the motivations and values of those directly involved in them. Staff and volunteers typically explained their own motivations in terms of their commitments to Law Centres' missions: 'meeting community needs for legal services' and concerns with 'addressing social justice issues', 'broadening access to quality advice' and 'access to justice for the most vulnerable in society', for example.

People's motivations are discussed in more detail in Chapter Eight, together with the ways in which motivations may have been shifting over time in response to changing contexts. Staff and volunteers brought values with them, and these values in turn were subject to modification. In some cases commitments deepened, while in other cases there was some evidence of erosion as people struggled with the dilemmas associated with the pressures of the Carter reform-related changes. The point to emphasise here is simply this, that the motivations and values of those who were working and volunteering in Law Centres were clearly linked to Law Centres' own ethos and values, whether as cause or effect – or both.

So what did staff consider to be the key aspects of Law Centres' ethos and values? There was broad agreement that the role of Law Centres was to facilitate access to justice for all, regardless of ability to pay or social position. It was about providing a "quality service ... to the people who can't access legal advice elsewhere". "There's no one else that helps the people we help", commented one Law Centre worker. The Law Centre was there to ensure that "all sections of the community [have] access to the law", a trustee remarked in similar vein. "We want to provide a quality service ... to the people who can't access legal advice elsewhere", a solicitor in another Law Centre said, emphasising the importance of quality provision.

Accessibility emerged in terms of locality and atmosphere, as well as in financial terms. The administrator in one Law Centre commented that the Law Centre that she managed was located in shop-front premises in an area of high social need. People could call into the Law Centre when going about their daily business.

Being physically accessible was seen to be important. A number of Law Centres were similarly located near to markets and local shops.

It was also recognised in one city, however, that there could be cases where clients might prefer to go to a more anonymous central location (if they were anxious to avoid relatives or neighbours learning that they were taking up issues of domestic violence, for example). In the city in question there were collaborative referral arrangements in place to address this issue. Issues of collaboration between different agencies are considered in more detail in Chapter Six.

The atmosphere in Law Centres was also seen as important, being welcoming to clients; "very approachable, informal", "clients like this", "they feel confident", as a local volunteer explained. A volunteer in another Law Centre made similar comments about the atmosphere, describing it as "so welcoming, so relaxed", with very helpful staff on the reception desk who were "so polite". If this hadn't been the case, she continued, "I wouldn't have bothered to give my time. I feel valued."

"We don't patronise people", a lawyer explained, adding that people could see this, "so we've built up a lot of trust" over the years. People "know that we're on their side." This chimes with the findings from earlier research which identified that less socially advantaged groups tended to prefer to obtain legal advice from a "one-sided" lawyer, that is, a lawyer who could be trusted to be on the side of the less-advantaged (Abel-Smith, Zander and Brooke, 1973).

A number of lawyers also commented on the importance of the atmosphere within the Law Centre in terms of team working and collective ways of working. One young woman noted, "I hadn't worked in one [collective] before ... it was a bit weird at first". She reflected that although it took some getting used to, it was positive to be treated with respect and to "feel valued" as part of the team. This was part of the Law Centre's ambience. In some instances experiences of working in such an atmosphere were contrasted with more negative past experiences , including in private practice, where the focus was described as being "there to make money for the boss".

However, there were also a few reflections on more negative experiences in Law Centres. Several lawyers contrasted the atmosphere in their current Law Centre with atmospheres that they had encountered elsewhere when collectives had not worked effectively or harmoniously. Law Centres were "special places", a Law Centre lawyer explained, "but they are only as special as the people in them. The ethos is constantly fragile and in need of what museum people call curation ... keeping the flame burning. The little flame can flicker and blow out", though.

The same lawyer elaborated on this theme: "one of the issues in terms of the fragility of the Law Centres is that the business case and the business realities are very different ... clearly one pressure on the ethic or ethos is the need to make it pay, to make it sustainable and to establish business disciplines on the work of each lawyer" – a balance that is increasingly difficult to manage, it was widely argued, and as later chapters illustrate in more detail. These issues about working relationships between staff, team working and the challenges of collective forms of organisation are explored in more detail in Chapter Five.

Law Centres were generally very busy – and sometimes working from unsuitable premises (with insufficient space for clients to speak with receptionists in privacy, for example). Some offices were also clearly in need of redecoration, being scruffy as well as cramped. The contrast with the décors of the private sector firms that were visited could scarcely have been more striking. But generally, and most importantly, Law Centre clients were observed being greeted in warm and welcoming ways. Typically, there were toys available for children and notice boards displaying information about a range of local services and community activities.

Holistic approaches

Another frequently emphasised aspect of Law Centres' ethos was the importance of treating clients' problems holistically. At this point, some clarification may be helpful, as the term 'holistic' was applied in two slightly different ways. When referring to an individual client, working 'holistically' implied addressing the client's different problems and needs comprehensively. For example, this might involve identifying the links between a client's presenting issue, such as the threat of eviction and consequent homelessness, and his or her underlying problems, such as problems with claiming welfare benefits, leading to debt and consequent rent arrears.

The term 'holistic' was also used to refer to collaboration between agencies, for example, providing 'holistic' services so that clients could be referred on to specialist agencies when appropriate. Chapter Six provides more detailed discussion of this latter usage of the term, exploring more generally the development of more collaborative approaches between different agencies across particular localities. In this chapter the focus is upon holistic approaches to working with individual clients.

"We're interested in the clients ... they are at the centre of what we do", explained the administrator of one Law Centre, adding that "we deal with vulnerable people" whose problems often overlapped. As a trustee in another Law Centre explained, the ethos was about providing "a seamless path". Others referred more specifically to the potential overlap between mental health problems and disability discrimination problems, for instance, or between benefits problems and rent arrears, or immigration problems and welfare benefits and housing problems. These types of problems needed time and patience to unravel and address. This was particularly so when a client also had mental health problems or language issues (needing an interpreter, for instance), which meant that even more time and patience would be required. A number of those who had had experience of working in private law firms suggested that Law Centres generally demonstrated far more patience when working with very vulnerable clients. Law Centre staff would also recognise that recovering relatively small sums (the example cited was of £900 in a compensation case) could make a vast to clients' lives if they were managing on a low income, even if such sums could seem trivial to private firms.

Other typical comments included similar reflections on the impact that Law Centres could make both for individuals' lives and for communities: "Making a difference ... allowing people to exercise their rights." "When I've done a case [successfully] I've changed someone's life", an immigration solicitor commented, explaining how asylum cases could and often did involve issues of life and death. The solicitor who made the last comment had previous experience of working in the private sector and drew comparisons between the ethos in each, while recognising that there were also individuals and firms that did share many of the Law Centres' values and demonstrated this by providing pro bono advice sessions, for instance.

Collective and preventative approaches to taking up common issues in the pursuit of social justice

Although there was general agreement that Law Centres were not set up to focus exclusively upon individual clients' cases, there were some variations in the emphasis given to the different aspects of this wider mission. Some highlighted the importance of pressing forward the law itself to promote social justice, taking test cases to strengthen legal rights for all (one lawyer described himself as a "legal guerrilla fighter" for social justice). Law Centres were able to use legal remedies to enforce rights – and to test and further develop rights – in ways that were beyond the scope of other advice agencies; a unique selling point in terms of their abilities to contribute to social justice agendas more widely.

Others emphasised the importance of community work in terms of public legal education and policy work, typically preventative work. And some highlighted each of these aspects. One person summarised this as: "The essence for me personally, it's about wider issues, to educate the local community and empower them [in relation to knowing and accessing their legal rights]". The Law Centre was concerned to "empower people to do it for themselves", a lawyer in another Law Centre similarly commented. There were a number of examples of test cases and of outreach and community-related work, including campaigning and public legal education that had been undertaken in the past.

One such example was of a campaign with Women in Prison that had generated a lot of work for a particular Law Centre. The campaign had been about trying to maintain inmates' homes while they were serving short-term prison sentences. This was seen as being very important so as to ensure that they had somewhere to go upon release. The campaign had resulted in some achievements .

Other examples of past policy work in other Law Centres had included taking up homeless people's problem of being unable to make contact with the office outside office hours, even when they needed emergency accommodation. Using the law to enforce the rights of homeless people, the Law Centre had enforced the provision of a 24-hour helpline by the council in question. Another example was the successful challenging of a council's policy of not giving reasons in writing for refusing accommodation to homeless people. Without reasons in writing it was very difficult to appeal a decision. As a result of the challenge, the policy was changed. But there was little if any time for this type of policy work under the current system, this Law Centre worker added.

Examples of test cases included one that had gone to the European Court of Human Rights in Strasbourg. This was a test case about immigration rules as they applied to a refugee who had temporary status but did not yet have settled status. If that person married outside the country before getting settled status, they could be refused the right of entry for their spouse. This was challenged as a violation of human rights. The Law Centre lawyer involved in the case explained that for him such cases were about "pushing the law to the boundaries" in the interests of justice.

He gave another example of a case that he had taken forward to push the boundaries. This was in relation to degrading treatment or torture, as applied to a Roma child with disabilities, and the child's access to appropriate education. At the tribunal the argument that the case involved degrading treatment had been accepted, in addition to the argument that it also involved the rights of the child. The lawyer explained that he had had the time and space to take this case effectively – and that such opportunities were what "really motivates".

An example from another Law Centre was of a case that had lasted for eight years, from the mid-1980s to 1992, ending up in the European Court of Human Rights. This case had forced a change in the law to clarify that the dismissal of a pregnant woman did indeed constitute sex discrimination. There were a number of other examples of test cases from a range of Law Centres taking up cases to clarify the law, to challenge discrimination and to extend rights in the interests of social justice.

These were precisely the types of approach that fitted most readily with the original Law Centre model – but least appropriately with the LSC funding system. "It's very hard to keep that initial ethos of the Law Centres going" while meeting these targets, a lawyer explained. They needed to organise campaigning, but there was no time to do this, he continued. "Even the simplest campaign would be difficult now." The experience of such pressures, and their impact on staff motivation, are explored in more detail in later chapters.

Law Centres' ethos: other stakeholders' perspectives

Meanwhile, to what extent were the claims that were being made by Law Centre staff and volunteers being reiterated by other stakeholders? There was broad agreement across other advice agencies, private sector providers, local authorities and other funders that Law Centres were making vital contributions in terms of enabling people to have access to justice, regardless of their inability to pay or other social disadvantages. The Law Centre was about "promoting equality, justice, access and fairness for people who wouldn't normally get access to legal advice and support", an advice worker in an ethnic minority community project reflected in one city. "Strongly value led", agreed an advice agency manager in another city, "with a strong fairness agenda" and ethical base that had impacted upon decisions taken in her own agency (such as the decision that representing landlords or employers would, in the agency's view, be in conflict with the commitment to work with tenants and employees).

Law Centres were seen as being "unequivocally there for the disadvantaged", in the view of an advice worker from another agency, who commented further that "the respect that local community groups have for the Law Centre is huge" and mentioned the Somali and Polish communities as examples.

"They want to help the most vulnerable", commented an advice worker about the Law Centre in a yet another city, who also pointed out that around two-thirds of the clients came from areas that were among the 20% most deprived localities in England. "The uniqueness of the Law Centre is that it is actually accessible to all", reflected an advice worker in another area. And "because it is a community-based organisation you see all sorts of people there. People can be intimidated by independent solicitors", she continued, "because they dress, they have a certain attire ... whereas the Law Centre's a lot more relaxed and [you can] express yourself a little bit more, being in that environment does make a difference." The atmosphere was "less formal and less intimidating than many private lawyers' offices", a lawyer providing pro bono advice sessions reflected in similar vein. "It's in a different style of seeing people", which made the Law Centre seem more accessible, in her view.

A former client explained how important this had all been to her, particularly commenting on the support she had received. She had been in what she described as "buckets of tears", but felt that she had been listened to with great sympathy as well as with professionalism. She did add that "I don't think the building is actually appropriate" (being in need of decoration and repair, in her view), but this in no way detracted from the warmth: "from the time you know you hit the door ... you could sense the warmth of the individuals in there".

The relatively informal atmosphere in Law Centres was in no way associated with a lack of professionalism, it was argued more widely. As an officer based in a funding agency commented: "Personally I value Law Centres very highly. I think the services they provide are amazing." Other stakeholders similarly commented on the quality of the services that Law Centres were providing. "At their best they're excellent", reflected an officer from a funding agency. Stakeholders, including those in private practice, spoke of their confidence in referring clients to their local Law Centre.

Stakeholders also commented on some of the challenges presented by Law Centre clients, many of whom required considerable time and patience to unravel their problems. An officer from a funding agency (with considerable personal experience of Law Centres) emphasised this preparedness "to spend time with clients, giving them that extra time and attention that makes them feel valued" and enabling their often related problems to be unpicked. An advice worker in an agency that collaborated closely with its local Law Centre similarly commented on the particular needs of both their client groups, "We are there for the people who don't manage", and added that this was a very "needy group". While the aim was to empower clients and to "work to promote independence", realistically this wasn't always possible, she added.

This willingness to give clients the time and attention needed to address their issues holistically was contrasted with the ethos in many private sector firms. They tended to be less patient, it was suggested, and particularly so in terms of tolerating challenging behaviours from clients with mental health and/or alcohol or substance abuse issues, for instance. A local councillor who had a background in private legal practice commented, "I can't tell you how different I think the two environments are", and explained that she had left private practice because "the underlying driver in a city firm is inevitably money" (although she added that there were, of course, private firms that provided pro bono legal advice, operating from a very different value basis, far closer to the values of Law Centres).

There were a number of similar comments contrasting the ethos in Law Centres with that in private firms. These included comments about the quality of the services provided by some private firms, in some localities, in particular areas of law.

There was one exception, however: a comment from a lawyer with experience of both private and not-for-profit sectors. She considered that clients were better treated as "a valuable commodity": "the whole level of courtesy is higher in private practice" in comparison with not-for-profit organisations, which tended to keep clients waiting if there was a queue. She pointed out that although it was important to listen to clients carefully and respond holistically, it was important to ask very focused questions and use time efficiently so as to get to the heart of the problem.

The benefits of Law Centres' local knowledge and policy inputs

In addition to the ways in which they treated individual clients, Law Centres' community base was also seen as an important factor, another of their unique selling points. "They have grassroots knowledge, which is a key to our local Law Centre", an advice worker in one city commented. This local community base was also valued by a number of local authority officers who commented on Law Centres' capacities, as a result, to contribute to policy development. One senior officer reflected that Law Centres could play an important role in improving decision making more generally. Through feedback from clients they could identify areas where administrative procedures were inadequate, for instance, providing valuable input. More systematic feedback, in this officer's view, could strengthen effective, outcomes-based accountability. Both the leader of the council and the chief executive were interested in promoting such aims, he added.

Very similar comments were made by local authority officers in other areas who expressed their appreciation of Law Centres that provided up-to-the minute feedback on clients' problems in the community as they arose. In one area the Law Centre was described as "one of our strongest partners", bringing clients' perspectives to strategic policy discussions. In this area the perspectives of people who were experiencing poverty were seen to be particularly important, given that the area had high levels of poverty and deprivation and that, as a result of the recession, the problems were spreading to affect previously less affected groups. Other examples of policy inputs included a review of homelessness in one city, jointly carried out between the CAB and the Law Centre, each focusing upon its particular areas of expertise.

There was also some appreciation of the fact that Law Centres and local authorities could and did find themselves in conflict over specific issues and cases. But this was not a reason for not funding Law Centres – on the contrary. One local authority officer reflected that at the back of officers' minds was the question "Why should I be paying you to sue me? It makes no sense in the short term."

However, he added that in the longer term, like complaints procedures in the private sector, this was "essential and integral. You learn from the challenges, those litigations, so it can help you improve your services, ensuring that those issues that have arisen do not arise again. It is more cost effective." As an officer in another local authority reflected, the independence of Law Centres was important within the wider context of the independent role of the third sector, the Centres being separate from the local authority and therefore being able to act against it, if need be, in the interests of clients/local people. While a number of local authorities clearly shared these views, this was certainly not universally the case, as Chapter Six considers in more detail.

Preventative approaches as part of Law Centres' original social justice mission

There was also widespread agreement over the potential importance of Law Centres' preventative work more generally. A local councillor commented that the local Law Centre in her area included work with families to avoid homelessness. This was to the benefit of the council (not having to pick up the tab) in addition to benefiting the families themselves. The Law Centre in that area also had a specific contract with the area's key social landlord to do preventative work. As a result of regular meetings with officers to identify problems and seek solutions as problems arose, the number of evictions had been reduced from around 300 cases per annum to around 50 cases annually. Rent arrears had been going down and tenant satisfaction scores had been going up. This was in "everyone's interest", being cost-effective as well as being effective in social terms.

The same councillor referred to the value of preventative work around education, challenging school exclusions. She pointed out that young people excluded from school were disproportionately at risk of unemployment and, indeed, of prison. Challenging unnecessary exclusions was therefore beneficial for society as well as for the young people concerned and their families.

An employment lawyer who provided pro bono advice sessions at another Law Centre stated that preventative work was being done in yet another area:

preventing tribunals from becoming clogged up. This was because, far from encouraging unrealistic claims, Law Centre staff gave clients very realistic advice, advising them not to pursue claims that were very unlikely to succeed. In this way Law Centres were contributing to the reduction of the work of tribunals. More generally (not specifically referring to employment law), a number of those interviewed also commented on the problems to be anticipated if fewer clients were represented and so decided to represent themselves. Magistrates and tribunal chairs typically much preferred clients to be represented, as this enabled cases to be heard more expeditiously.

But, as Law Centre staff and volunteers had noted, under LSC funding systems there was less scope for preventative work, or for policy work, community work or public legal education, unless funding could be obtained via separate sources. There were some fictions, in any case, about Law Centres' wider role, which "wasn't as prevalent as it should be", as one lawyer put it. While the local Law Centre had in the past had a high profile in terms of campaigning on homelessness policies and procedures, on housing conditions such as damp and on racial harassment, a local authority officer commented, this wasn't necessarily so evident in the current context.

Similar points were made about Law Centres' wider roles in terms of public legal education and training, community outreach work and capacity building. Here too, some of the public legal education and training work that was going on was being facilitated as a result of separate project funding. Otherwise, in the view of a senior advice worker who reflected upon her knowledge of a number of Law Centres, they had "shifted away from this" because of the pressures of the funding system for legal aid, even if they still espoused this wider role in principle. Stakeholders certainly referred to examples of past test cases, as the previous section has illustrated. But such cases seemed to be a diminishing feature of Law Centres' work in more recent times.

There were anxieties about a possible loss of vision more generally, as those more directly involved also recognised, and fears that, in their struggles to meet the requirements of the current funding system, Law Centres might be drifting away from their original mission. "It's very very hard", commented a solicitor. "I think in terms of [being] an employee it really demotivated me ... we had to move away from perhaps more complicated work where we could try and change policy with local authorities", she added, giving an example of preventative work on tenants' housing issues. "You know you want to help people", she continued, "you want to help the community, you are there because you don't want to make profit like a private firm, you want to make a difference and it seems that the government is trying to squeeze that out of the community." The solicitor in question was in the process of moving on from a Law Centre to work for another not-for-profit organisation. This leads us into a more detailed discussion of the changes that have been taking place and the challenges that these changes have posed for Law Centres' ethos and values – the subject of following chapters.

FOUR

Challenges and dilemmas

The previous chapter described Law Centres, their ethos and values, setting the context for the discussion of the impact of the Carter reforms to legal aid. As Chapter Two has already illustrated, these reforms were the subject of considerable debate when they were first proposed. Critics predicted that the results would be damaging in a number of ways, potentially undermining poor people's access to justice and posing challenges and dilemmas for those engaged in providing legal aid services. This chapter starts by summarising some of the evidence that has emerged as the reforms have been implemented. This sets the context for considering the impact on Law Centres more specifically. How did their staff and volunteers experience these changes, what challenges were posed and what dilemmas emerged? As the final section of this chapter points out, while the Carter reforms were initially the major focus of concern, subsequent proposals for legislative changes to legal aid became a more immediate focus, and posed threats to much of legal aid funding. Later chapters explore in further detail the challenges and dilemmas that were exacerbated as a result of the changes.

Recent research findings

Research studies on the impact and meaning of changes to the provision of legal aid since the early 1990s have argued that the results have been 'an irresistible pressure towards routine, poor quality justice' (Sommerlad, 2008, p 179) and that opposition to the reforms was 'pilloried as the product of either self-interest or naivety' (Sommerlad, 2008, p 182). While claims of self-interest may have some validity, what Sommerlad argued was that the reforms were undermining relationships based upon reciprocity and trust, substituting these for social relations that 'entailed the micro regulation of the legal aid practitioner' (Sommerlad, 2008, p 183). The end result was that professional autonomy was undermined and increasing gulfs emerged between corporate firms, on the one hand, and those undertaking legal aid work, on the other, mirroring the inequalities in their client bases and, hence, in society at large (Sommerlad, 2008).

The focus upon competition and entrepreneurialism had perverse effects, potentially reducing the supply of quality services for clients, it was argued. "[T]he margins are so tight ... and there are constant changes", a senior partner commented, "you just get exhausted". In his view, this distracted from building up a business plan, which was "a farce anyway because the goal posts are moved and moved and moved". This could result in firms deciding that it was 'no longer economically rational to practice legal aid' (Sommerlad, 2008, p 184).

For practitioners, the changes resulted in loss of morale. Increasing marketisation led to increasing competition, which 'creates bad feeling among people who used to be colleagues' rather than 'promoting networking and collaboration'. And the dissection of professional knowledge/work 'and its recomposition into precise, standardized (and hence measurable) tasks and sets of technical skills ... was viewed as primarily designed to achieve control of professional labour and thereby cut costs'. As a result, "There is virtually no time for a human dimension or real diagnosis", a lawyer commented (Sommerlad, 2008, p 185).

In summary, Sommerlad concluded, marketisation was leading to increasingly unequal outcomes. While recognising that access to justice in an adversarial system may be expensive, these reforms targeted access for the poor, while the law remained 'an essential resource for the powerful' (Sommerlad, 2008, p 190). Corporate lawyers were doing well, while legal aid lawyers were feeling increasingly squeezed.

Recent research has uncovered the impact of the changes on Law Centres. James and Killick's study of legal aid practitioners based in a Law Centre identified the dilemmas that they faced in the context of their work on immigration cases (James and Killick, 2010). The caseworkers whom James and Killick interviewed found themselves 'caught in the middle between these ever increasing financial pressures and their ethical obligations to their clients' (James and Killick, 2010, p 13). While all of those studied had 'a commitment, a belief in the importance of what they are doing', the authors argued, 'many have begun to talk of disillusionment with the system and weariness of the increasing pressures to work faster and deal with more clients, with a concomitant diminution in the quality of the advice and service they can offer' (James and Killick, 2010, p 13). However worthy the intentions of policies to ensure value for money and accountability for public funds, the actual result of the reforms to legal aid appeared to be 'undermining universal access to expert legal advice, a vital element in personalizing what can otherwise be a dehumanizing bureaucracy' (in this particular case, the Border Agency) (James and Killick, 2010, p 14).

Challenges and dilemmas for Law Centres

There are echoes of all of these arguments in relation to Law Centres, starting with the challenges inherent in the Carter reforms' fixed fees system, the administrative systems involved and their operation in practice. These were seen as being problematic for staff, resulting in negative effects on services to clients. There were also concerns with the impact of the Carter reforms in terms of reducing the scope for Law Centres to carry out their wider functions in communities, such as public legal education and training and other aspects of preventative work. Taken together, the changes were resulting in tensions and stress.

While these challenges were at the forefront, a number of staff referred to other stress-inducing factors, including the rising demand for legal advice as a result of increasing indebtedness and as a result of changes in public policies, such as those relating to social welfare law and immigration. It should also be emphasised once again that the focus was shifting, as Law Centres and other stakeholders faced the potential challenges of proposed legislation that would remove a number of key areas of the law from the scope of legal aid. However challenging it had been to provide legal aid *within* the context of the LSC's funding system, it would be even more challenging to try to continue to provide services *without* legal aid funding in these areas of the law.

Financial and administrative challenges

Unsurprisingly, given the findings from other studies of legal aid provision more generally, the fixed fees system was identified as a challenge, because it did not cover the true costs of much, if not most, of Law Centres' casework. While exceptional cases did qualify for a higher rate, most of Centres' cases fell in between the basic and the exceptional case categories. As a result, there were pressures to focus upon particular types of cases, either the simplest or the most complex. This put a squeeze on the middle-level cases such as homelessness reviews, it was argued.

The LSC was clear that there should not be 'cherry picking' of cases to take account of these pressures, as an administrator in one Law Centre reflected. But in practice Law Centres were finding it very difficult to handle all potential cases. So, for example, the employment lawyer in one Law Centre commented that it could not handle employment discrimination cases because these tended to take too long. The Law Centre did try to get a balance of cases, but was "torn between the devil and the deep blue sea". There were felt to be pressures for a quick turnaround, on the one hand, versus the pressures of community needs, on the other (including the need for test cases to be taken up).

As a worker from another Law Centre commented, the ethos was such that there was a great reluctance to turn people away, "particularly because we don't get enough money out of their case", which "would be an awful reason to turn someone away". The system was effectively turning Law Centres into behaving "much more like a private firm", "having to be much more strategic about the cases we take on" and potentially leaving a great many people without effective access to justice, seeing a "pounds and pence sign" over the heads of potential clients as they walked through the door, as another staff member expressed their fears. There were similar comments from the administrator of a different Law Centre, who reflected that it had needed to work "smarter" and spend less time with individual clients in order to meet the challenges of the funding system for legal aid. Staff with experience of private practice had been able to provide advice and support on this point, being more aware of and used to private sector approaches in general, and to time management and recording time spent with each client more specifically.

An officer from a funding agency commented that Law Centres' preparedness and effectiveness in pursuing cases, "taking cases in order to win them for people that need this rather than to earn money from the legal aid system", was, ironically, one of the reasons for Law Centres' financial problems and why they were threatened with going broke. In his view, this was not the most effective way to get the most money from legal aid. The system of cost per case was riddled with perverse incentives, he concluded.

Meanwhile, others pointed out that the fixed fee system was also problematic in terms of the lack of provision for maintaining and renewing overheads, such as computing equipment. In several Law Centres the lack of up-to-date equipment was evident and added to the administrative pressures on staff. This was particularly difficult to manage, as the Legal Services Commission's administrative requirements were viewed as complex and frequently changing – an issue that was frequently cited as presenting challenges for Law Centre staff. A trustee in one Law Centre commented in similar vein. She had attended a half-day training course for trustees but still found the administration very complicated in practice, as did the staff (despite having extensive previous experience as a manager in other public service sector agencies).

The new administrative requirements were complex and the computer system very difficult, and quotas changed from month to month. Compiling the returns was very stressful, according an administrator in one Law Centre: "worse than PMT". And the financial arrangements were viewed as being very unsatisfactory in other ways too. It was very difficult to plan because income varied from month to month. There were also problems with the process of bidding for a new contract. The term 'Byzantine' was used on a number of occasions, to describe different aspects of the administrative processes involved.

The Legal Services Commission's comments, in contrast

From the LSC's perspective, the administrative requirements could be experienced as challenging but were actually no more so, and possibly rather less so, than the requirements of other agencies managing government contracts. Had the requirements to become more 'business-like' posed tensions and dilemmas for these other agencies? From the LSC's perspective some Law Centres had not been adequately prepared for the changes, it was suggested. But this was the reality that had to be faced if legal aid resources were to be used most cost-effectively so as to maximise the throughput of cases and reach the maximum number of eligible clients.

Law Centres needed to manage themselves effectively – as some were – and as some were learning from the experiences of others that were succeeding in working with the fixed fees system. Financial incompetence was unacceptable. Arguments about the difficulty/impossibility of operating viably within the fixed fee system when working with diverse groups of clients did not stack up, in the LSC's view, given that some providers in diverse areas could operate viably within the fixed fee system. For example, it was not necessary to use qualified lawyers for every type of case and simpler cases could be handled by paralegal staff (working under legal supervision). This was considered to be more cost-effective.

There was no overall shortage of those seeking to bid for tenders, which indicated to the LSC that the fixed fee system was not actually deterring potential providers, at least in urban areas. The implication was that Law Centres that were finding this all so difficult could usefully learn from the experiences of others that were successfully providing legal aid within the requirements of the fixed fee system. This could be achieved by becoming more business-like, it was argued.

Law Centre perspectives, in response

Becoming more business-like was clearly being required, then. But at what costs? As has already been suggested, there was evidence that some staff were now applying their previous experience of working in private firms, including more business-like ways of organising and managing time, to their present work contexts. Chapter Five examines this issue in further detail, identifying some of the resulting dilemmas for Law Centres striving to survive in this more business-like context – but without losing sight of their mission and ethos, and avoiding becoming market-dominated in the process.

While some Law Centre staff and volunteers were evidently confident that they had worked out how to operate successfully within the LSC's requirements, others expressed serious reservations, including about their independence as legal aid professionals. "The independence is sacrificed ... the flexibility, the ability to work in the way that you want to a reasonable extent is an absolute prerequisite of the independence of a lawyer", one lawyer argued. "A lawyer that has to say: 'I can't do any more because my funder won't pay me any more' is not a lawyer who is independent. A lawyer who has to work on that case but not this aspect of it ... if it's a debt aspect or if it's a benefit aspect, a housing aspect, an employment aspect and you do this and not that, all because of the dictates of the funder, that's not an independent lawyer. That's not a proper public legal service and that's what [has] happened to community law", the same lawyer concluded.

Law Centres that were less dependent upon LSC funding were better placed to cope with these challenges, it was pointed out, having more flexibility to respond to needs that fell outside the LSC's criteria in terms of eligibility for funding. But reductions in local authority expenditure were widely anticipated (local authorities having been significant funders for a number of Law Centres, as explained in Chapter Two). There was likely to be increasing competition for funding, including funding from charitable trusts, and "every year the cake is getting smaller", it was recognised.

Meanwhile, demand for services was increasing and was likely to increase further as a result of public policy changes such as the (then) forthcoming changes to housing benefit (which were expected to lead to increasing problems with homelessness) and in other parts of the benefits system. A Law Centre advice worker summarised the potential effects as "It's going to be chaotic". Others stated that the law had been becoming increasingly complex in any case, adding further challenges. This applied to a number of areas of the law, including immigration.

Rapid changes also potentially posed challenges in terms of administrative decisions, it was argued, leading to poor administrative decision making. One lawyer suggested that spending on legal aid might be reduced simply by improving the quality of decision making in areas such as social welfare law and immigration law, as this would reduce the number of challenges to be made.

Legal aid, in the view of another lawyer, was focused upon going to court: "it is all about dealing with things that have gone wrong". He contrasted this with the role that Law Centres ought to be playing, acting in more preventative ways: "not having to raise a grievance, but knowing your rights", so that people could take these up in a self-confident and informed way. "If people are empowered at the front end of these processes then they don't have to resort to litigation later", he added. This theme of the value of preventative and policy work is explored more fully in Chapter Seven.

An officer from a funding agency argued that Law Centres were prepared to "spend time with clients", "giving them that extra time and attention that makes them feel valued", enabling their often linked/complex problems to be unpicked. As he pointed out, however, "legal aid doesn't pay for this" aspect of Law Centres' approach – that of identifying and addressing clients' problems holistically rather than taking each issue separately and as rapidly as possible. "At their best, they [Law Centres] change lives", he explained, "they get people completely out of the hole that they're in and mend them." "They become self-sufficient, ceasing to cost the state money."

In one Law Centre, for example, outreach sessions were being provided at a local community centre in order to reach women from particular ethnic minority communities in "their own space", where translation facilities were also available. These were precisely the types of activities that were not covered by the fixed fee system. Later chapters explore in more detail both these issues and the related dilemmas that they posed for Law Centre staff and volunteers.

Exploring potential clients' eligibility for legal aid under the fixed fees system was a particularly sensitive issue for a number of Law Centres. Some Law Centres preferred not to demand proof of eligibility from potential clients before they could be seen, even though this sometimes involved more work subsequently, in order to provide the relevant evidence for the LSC. Other Law Centres displayed prominent notices explaining the need to bring evidence of eligibility. This was an issue that required sensitive handling, however, if Law Centres' reputations for accessibility were not to be undermined.

One administrative worker explained: "I need to check people's eligibility. I need to ask them to bring documents on their first visit ... to prove ... as some sort of proof of income", which saves time, as clients don't then have to return, "or might not return with their documents". "In a way it does make it more efficient", she said, but at the risk of diverting from "the problem that arrives through the door". She tried to be discreet, she explained, "to make sure that they don't feel they are being judged in any way ... but also I don't always have the time to reassure them that if they don't have the right income they will still be seen". (This particular Law Centre had funding from the local authority that enabled staff to provide at least some advice before filtering out those who did not fit the LSC criteria for eligibility.)

A number of those interviewed also expressed concern about the potential clients whose incomes/resources were such that they were just above the eligibility criteria. They would be unable to afford private solicitors, and so would effectively be denied access to justice because of their inability to pay. Such situations were likely to increase, it was pointed out, if legal aid were to become even more restricted along the lines of the legislation that was being debated in Parliament at the time.

Education, training and development

As previous chapters have already explained, another of the particular distinguishing features of Law Centres was their ability to provide specialist services and to provide training for 'first tier' (that is, front-line) advice agencies working in partnership with them and supporting agencies such as Citizens' Advice Bureaux (CABs), which would refer complex cases to the Law Centres. This was over and above the public legal education work that Law Centres had been carrying out in community-based organisations, schools and prisons, for example. But the funding system was not conducive to this type of approach either. As one administrative worker described the situation in one Law Centre, it was "living hand to mouth". Public legal education and training were among the aspects of the work that were being squeezed as a result of the pressures, although there were still collaborative relationships with the CAB (which had decided not to compete in bidding for contracts). This particular Law Centre still managed to provide regular training sessions for referral agencies, in order to update them on changes in welfare law. But this was not the case all round. A member of staff in another Law Centre commented that it was essential to keep up to date, "to be at the cutting edge", both for its own clients and to provide specialist advice to other agencies. But its internal training budget had suffered and there were reduced resources for training work with other agencies.

While these types of comment about reductions in opportunities for education and training were widespread, it did emerge that there were still examples of good practice in these respects. There were examples of collaboration, where Law Centres were providing specialist advice and supporting other advice agencies, for instance. Chapter Six addresses these aspects of Law Centres' work and future strategies in more detail.

Another impact of the Carter reforms was the reduction of funding to provide legal training, widening access to the legal profession. Law Centres had provided progression routes in these ways, enabling former clients, volunteers and administrative staff to qualify as lawyers themselves. While the numbers were relatively small, it emerged that these types of opportunities had been particularly helpful for members of ethnic minority communities, enabling them to pursue careers in the law. Examples of the importance of such opportunities are provided in Chapter Eight.

Resulting tensions, dilemmas and stress

Both staff and management committee members provided illustrations of how stressful the changes actually were, in their experience. Being in what felt like a "state of crisis" was stressful in any event. People spoke of feeling trapped by the challenges of survival from day to day, without the time to focus upon longer-term solutions. "We're in a very very difficult situation", reflected a member of staff in a Law Centre that was facing possible closure. "I don't want to work anywhere else; I want to work in this organisation", he continued. "But I'm obviously very very worried about the next three months."

Insecurity emerged as a major source of stress. One young lawyer reflected that "this has to be a big problem". As a young person, she said, "you think, could this job sustain me?" Although she felt that she was getting excellent guidance and support and was very positive about working in the Law Centre, she explained that "I'm worried about the future". Others similarly pointed to what they identified as "worrying levels of stress" as a result of these insecurities.

While so many of the stresses that loomed large for staff and volunteers related to the then-current funding context, it is important to recognise that these were not the only sources of tension. There were several examples of stresses related to staffing issues, for instance, including conflicts within collectives (if collectives found it difficult to address performance issues, for example). Where individuals had come into collectives without being fully committed to collective ways of working this had given rise to particular challenges, collectives not necessarily being geared towards managing such problems effectively. This had generational dimensions, it was suggested, some younger members of staff having grown up with more individualistic orientations and correspondingly less understanding of – or even sympathy with – more collective approaches. This issue of the extent to which there were indeed generational differences is explored in more detail later in this chapter and in Chapter Eight.

There were, in addition, examples of conflicts of interest within and between communities as well as between staff, including issues where allegations of racism had been involved. As in other studies, conflicts involving allegations of racism have been some of the most painful issues to be addressed within teams and within communities (Hoggett et al, 2009).[1]

Chapter Eight explores some of these issues in more depth, examining the stresses that were identified as a result of the challenges faced and the dilemmas that were posed for Law Centre staff and volunteers. Later chapters also reflect on the survival strategies that were being adopted as Law Centre staff and volunteers strove to safeguard access to justice for all – coping with the pressures to become more "business-like", as a number of those interviewed expressed it – without jeopardising their underlying ethos and values.

Meanwhile there was widespread recognition that Law Centres were "going into difficult times", implying the need for "hard and difficult decisions". A number of possible survival strategies were proposed – strategies that were subsequently also recommended by a Cabinet Office report on ways forward for not-for-profit advice services in England more generally, in the context of rising demands and diminishing resources to meet them (Cabinet Office, 2011). But many of these strategies were highly contentious, posing further ethical dilemmas for those involved. For example, various forms of charging for services had been identified as a possibility that might be explored with the Law Society. While this might generate income and provide relatively accessible services to those who were ineligible for legal aid but unable to afford a private solicitor, there were anxieties that "this might be when it starts undermining the principles. How far do you go down that road – who should pay and who should not pay? There are so many tensions at the moment."

Other possible options included developing partnership working with private solicitors (already established in some cases, in relation to pro bono work for instance, although in other geographical areas there was a dearth of lawyers providing pro bono services). Another option involved taking on "no win no fee work" (although there were anxieties that this could lead to "ambulance chasing"). There was also some discussion of the option of setting up a trading arm, to take on for-profit work in the city centre, for example, in order to develop ways of cross-subsidising the Law Centre's main work elsewhere with disadvantaged communities. "I personally don't think this would be a step too far", one lawyer commented, although recognising that "a lot of people would disagree with that". (In the event, a number of social enterprises were subsequently being developed.)

Others referred to potential practical difficulties, as well as raising more fundamental objections in principle to such proposals. Law Centres have been operating in very different contexts, covering both urban and rural areas, providing services across different aspects of the law. Potential solutions such as charging for some services, setting up a social enterprise trading arm, developing partnerships with other agencies and with private solicitors, increasing the scope for pro bono work and increasing the use of volunteers in partnership with local universities may have been feasible to pursue in some contexts (as subsequent experiences demonstrated), but were simply impractical in others.

While some of those involved with Law Centres expressed clear views either for or against such proposals, in principle (rather than simply in practice) others were less decided. "We are open to anything" to keep the Law Centre's services going, it was suggested in one Law Centre, for example. If one or more of its particular areas of the law were taken out of funding, then alternatives would have to be explored. The current uncertainty was "terribly draining though", taking its toll on morale. But expressions of willingness to be open to anything were accompanied by expressions of specific reservations. The Law Centre in question would not consider taking on cases for employers or landlords, for instance, as this would be seen as being incompatible with the Law Centre's ethos.

A number of dilemmas were faced, then, by those involved with Law Centres, with parallels with the dilemmas faced by those concerned with the provision of public services and with the public service ethos more generally. Some discussed the varying ways in which they would reach decisions about such possible developments, how they would set about drawing their own personal bottom lines, balancing the need to operate in business-like ways with the importance of holding on to their professional values and the Law Centres' ethos. One trustee (with extensive experience of public sector management across a range of different service areas) also explained, however, that this sometimes felt like drawing lines in the sand, and drew parallels with the ways in which public attitudes had shifted more generally over time – citing the widespread acceptance of police officers carrying guns, for example. What had seemed unacceptable at one time could subsequently become the norm, she pointed out. There were continuing dilemmas here, involving emotional labour on an on-going basis, as later chapters explore in more detail.

Note
[1] This has been the personal experience of the lead author in a number of different contexts over the years.

FIVE

Public service modernisation, restructuring and recommodification

'The shifting boundary between private and public responsibility for social welfare is one of the *longue durée* stories of Western history', a number of commentators have suggested (Drakeford, 2008, p 163). As previous chapters have pointed out, the shift towards greater public responsibility after the Second World War met with a concerted check following the election of the Thatcher government 1979 and the Regan administration in 1980. The future was to be one of 'customers not clients, purchasers not providers, managers not administrators, competition not allocation, regulation not planning and equality of opportunity not equality of outcome' (Drakeford, 2008, p 163).

New Labour came to power in 1997 with the promise of modernising the welfare state rather than further privatising it. Yet public service modernisation policies continued aspects of neoliberal policy, it has already been argued, attempting to use social policy to complement rather than to challenge market imperatives (Page, 2007). As Chapter One has already pointed out, public service modernisation was also accompanied by the increasing use of performance targets and the promotion of private sector audit and management practices.

These forms of restructuring have typically impacted upon staff pay and conditions (Whitfield, 2006), potentially undermining staff morale. They have also been associated with the deskilling of professionals, reducing the scope for the use of professional judgement. Standing has described these processes in terms of 'occupational dismantling' – an 'onslaught' on the professions that is associated with neoliberal agendas more widely (Standing, 2011, pp 38–9).

While critics have pointed to the potentially negative implications for public service professionals and their clients, they have also pointed to the continuing scope for human agency (Newman and Clarke, 2009). Public service modernisation has been implemented in varying ways in different contexts. As Barnes and Prior also suggested, both professional practitioners and citizens have the capacity for counter-agency, as potentially 'subversive citizens' (Barnes and Prior, 2009, p 22). But counter-agency is not without its costs. 'Managing the volatile intersection of needs, choices, resources and competing priorities will remain a site of intense emotional labour', it has been argued (Clarke, Smith and Vidler, 2006, p 159). How do these debates apply to Law Centre staff and volunteers in the context of the Carter reforms and subsequent proposals for change?

This chapter examines the impacts on Law Centres' decision-making processes and structures and their accountability systems, as well as the impacts on staff pay and conditions in the more competitive climate. The flat organisational structures of Law Centres, including flat pay structures, collective decision-making processes and community representation have been under pressure. The chapter concludes by focusing upon the particular issue of whether – and, if so, how – Law Centres' should charge clients for services, a controversial issue that in some ways epitomises the dilemmas that Law Centres have been facing as they strive to survive in a competitive market while maintaining their underlying ethos and social purpose.

The Carter reforms and the new managerialism

The introduction of competitive tendering was accompanied by performance-related targets, posing new challenges for Law Centres used to operating in very different ways, as the previous chapter has outlined. As the chief executive of one of a Law Centre's partner agencies reflected, in his view the LSC had "bought into New Labour's performance management culture to an excessive degree", losing sight of customer care in the process. "It just went mad", he added, "with a macho culture which entirely lost sight of what the organisation was there to do", at some levels within the organisation, although not at the top of the LSC, he continued, the leadership being committed to access to justice, in his view. A long-serving member of staff reflected, in parallel, that the Law Centre in question had gone "from being a provider of a social service, even though we are providing legal advice and being a charity in that sense, to being a business".

A recurring theme was how to avoid undermining the Law Centre's mission by "operating like a production line", a "factory approach" as one Law Centre lawyer expressed it, in order to meet the LSC's requirements to obtain the maximum throughput of clients. Legal aid work was "not like Tesco's – it's not like selling baked beans", he continued.

The pressures of centrally defined targets were similar to those experienced by local authorities and by other voluntary agencies more generally, of course, including those providing advice and related services. The chief executive of one such agency commented that "If you high perform you're going to attract a lot of funding and when you have a lot of funding you can then deliver other things" – and vice versa. So Law Centres "need to evolve and see themselves as a brand and as a market" in order to attract more resources and so be in a position to meet their social justice objectives. "Advice provision can become very commercial; Law Centres need to be aware of that", he concluded.

This all required a very different approach, it was suggested. "The challenge for Law Centres is that they are going to have to become very very innovative ... they've got to change their model like we have had to and they can't continue with their socialist collective model", was the view of an advice worker in a voluntary sector agency that had a collaborative relationship with another Law Centre. "We are led by a very business-minded director", she continued, and while he was driven by principles of community service, "he is business-minded first and foremost", submitting funding bids and bidding for competitive tenders. Such arguments were not lost on a number of Law Centres, which decided that flat management structures and collective working practices were no longer viable. Staffing structures needed to be revisited, along with staff pay and conditions, while they strove to maintain their Law Centre's overall ethos, supported by effective team working.

Collective working

Collective working had been typical of Law Centres' operation. In some cases this had involved commitment to formal parity of positions and pay. In other cases there was equality in terms of participation in decision making, but disparities in terms of pay, depending upon levels of qualification and skill, for instance. There were, in fact, a range of models, with variations over time. What these differing arrangements had in common, though, was a shared commitment to democratic ways of working, a commitment that stood in marked contrast to the hierarchical systems associated with the New Public Management.

Although these forms of collective working had been much-valued features of many Law Centres' ethos from the early days, as previous chapters have already indicated, collective ways of working were appreciated by some newer members of staff too. Working in a collective way had taken some getting used to, several commented, but it was seen as very positive to be treated with respect and "to feel valued", as part of the team. A staff member in one Law Centre reflected that when she had first taken up her post she had found it difficult, if not impossible, to contribute to team discussions, having been used to a hierarchy in the private sector where the boss gave instructions without asking staff for their views. Now she contributed freely to team discussions, taking "the bull by the horns" to raise issues openly. In her view, this collective approach to working was an important aspect of the Law Centre's ethos, and it was important in terms of its effectiveness too. She gave an example to illustrate the point. Around four years previously there had been a threat of local council funding cuts. The staff had "all really pulled together as a collective" strategically, as a result of which they had succeeded in maintaining their funding – at least for the time being.

Given the value that had been placed on collective ways of working, it was unsurprising that moving away from this had been experienced as very negative, in a number of cases. Relatively recently, for example, one Law Centre had changed from being a collective (in response to the need to address the implications of the Carter changes), but this shift had been experienced as problematic and the arrangement "didn't really work". The manager, who subsequently took over, reflected that "demoralisation has been substantial" among the staff, as a result.

In another Law Centre the decision to move from a collective to a more traditional organisational structure had actually been reversed. It moved from being a collective to having a hierarchy for a couple of years, but this had not worked so well. It therefore reverted to the collective, and this had been maintained over the last 10 years or so. Any administrative problems or policy issues were normally dealt with in staff meetings. While the LSC's requirements were described as being

---

"administratively a pain", the staff considered that "we do [this] quite well" here, despite the constant changes to the LSC's rules.

While collective ways of working had been very positively valued, there were also examples of more negative experiences, as previous chapters have already indicated. Working in Law Centres where collectives had not been functioning effectively had evidently been frustrating and, on occasions, painful experiences. If individuals lacked commitment, collectives could find it extremely difficult to handle the associated performance management issues. One lawyer described the first Law Centre in which he had worked many years previously as "a cantankerous and argumentative collective mismanaged by a local management committee that had no concept of how to drive a Law Centre. The whole thing was dysfunctional to the extreme and actually fell to pieces about a year after [an unnamed individual involved in management committee] left and had to be rescued", he reflected, adding that this Law Centre had indeed been effectively rescued and was "now a wholly different organisation".

The shift from collective to more traditional management structures was actually experienced positively in some cases. As one manager described this, the Law Centre was addressing the challenges while the staff was described as being "on side". They were actually relieved not to have responsibility for tendering and financial management. "This lets them get on with the job they want to do", the manager explained, a view that was fully corroborated by the staff in question. A lawyer in another Law Centre similarly explained that she was now the co-director, a position that was developed some four or five years earlier, following the decision to move away from a collective organisational structure. The collective had been a positive way to work in many ways. "It was lovely in the '70s and '80s", she added. But there simply wasn't time to operate in the collective mode now, given the increasing pressures. Although the decision to shift from the collective structure had been the subject of some discussion at the time, there had not been too much conflict. In her view, people were now happy, being able to come in and get on with their work, and leaving others to manage the financial and administrative pressures that the Law Centre was facing.

Comparable views were expressed by a very experienced lawyer in a Law Centre with a long tradition of working as a collective. This Law Centre did not have a formal hierarchy but had brought in a part-time administrator with directly relevant experience. "He's fantastic", the lawyer commented. Nobody had wanted to take on the managerial responsibilities and he had taken them on very effectively, in her view greatly benefiting the Law Centre as a result. This seemed to combine the benefits of effective administration with the strengths of good team working.

There were similar examples of such successful combinations in a number of other Law Centres, including one Law Centre that had recently appointed an administrator while maintaining a collective approach to overall decision-making. Having resisted such a move for a long time, the staff in this Law Centre still saw themselves as working collectively – as the recently appointed administrator explained, he was the administrator working with the collective, not the "manager", and the staff would be deeply resistant to his being described as the latter. It was similarly argued by the chief executive of a partner agency that it was essential to have leadership, whether the person concerned was called a manager or something else, and he added that "even in a collective it's down to leadership"; whatever the job title, that person needed to provide leadership and, most importantly, to have the necessary authority and the confidence of the staff. There were examples, then, of Law Centres successfully combining a clear management structure with democratic team working in practice.

In summary, moving from one type of organisational structure to another, to become more business-like, had been extremely challenging in a number of cases. As one trustee reflected on the process overall, quoting the example of redundancies as having been particularly problematic, it had been "a hard road". "But the question again is do you want to continue", he added. "It's all about survival ... sometimes an organisation has to adapt to survive. People don't necessarily welcome this ... but sometimes you have to take hard choices ...it's not a position that anybody would like to be in but ... we do want to be here today and tomorrow." "It's like a hot air balloon", he concluded, "you just have to drop some sandbags. We've done that and we've faced up to that."

Staffing structures

Staffing structures had also needed to be addressed. As one Law Centre manager commented, Law Centres tended to be seen as "top heavy with lawyers" in comparison with caseworkers. While this might have benefits for clients (being seen initially by the most experienced staff, who were well equipped to diagnose their problems effectively), it did not "sit easily with the funding system for legal aid". On the contrary, in fact, the LSC's view was that simpler cases could be handled effectively by paralegal staff working under professional legal supervision, as previous chapters have already indicated. Journal articles had examined the ways in which such staffing systems were being deployed (Makepeace, 2009) and had provoked some controversy about different business models among those concerned with the provision of civil legal aid services (Scott-Moncrieff, 2010).

It has been argued that there were parallels here with the polarisation that was being identified in other professions, while 'the legal profession is undergoing the most profound restructuring (the use of paraprofessionals having been described as providing cheap, standardized "Tesco law") all professions are being pushed in the same direction, of having fewer protected insiders alongside a growing number of insecure career-less positions' (Standing, 2011, p 50).

The solution of using paralegal caseworkers was being adopted, even in a Law Centre that described itself as having "held out as long as we could" against the trend. But it was described as having become inevitable in the current financial climate, so that in this particular Law Centre caseworkers were being employed and were paid less than experienced lawyers. While lawyers continued to be self-servicing in some Law Centres (doing their own filing, for example), these practices were also shifting in other Centres, with some staff trying to take on more of the background administrative work in order to free up the lawyers to concentrate on the more specialist legal aspects of the work.

Staffing costs, pay and conditions

Different views were also expressed about the pay and conditions of Law Centre staff, and the extent to which these could or should be restructured. One view was that many Law Centre staff were actually relatively well paid, with conditions of employment that compared favourably with those of other public sector employees. This was the view of one administrator, for instance, who felt that it could not be justified in the current climate. Redundancies might also have to be explored, he said, adding that "we're not going to look the same as we do now", in the future.

Others expressed very different views, however. While some Law Centres were considered to have had relatively favourable pay and conditions in the past, there was also evidence that some staff were earning considerably less than they would have been earning elsewhere, whether in the private or the public sector. For instance, one lawyer explained that she would have been earning almost double her current salary if she had continued to work as a legal officer with the local authority. Another explained similarly that she had taken a significant pay cut, moving from an academic job to work at her local Law Centre, and added that she was in a position to do this because her family was now self-supporting. Lawyers were not necessarily comparatively well paid, then, although relatively flat pay structures may well have been more favourable for support staff in some Law Centres.

The issue in relation to redundancies, as one trustee explained, was the question of "are we treating them fair" ... "have their rights been taken into account ... has the criterion been fair ... and if there were alternatives have we considered them?" This trustee was only too aware that the staff in question had been producing what he described as "quality stuff". A judge had recently commended one of the solicitors on the quality of the preparation for a case, for instance. But it was perhaps no longer feasible to give any one case such detailed time and attention in future, in the trustee's view.

As an alternative approach to containing staffing costs, salary cuts had been applied in some cases, both in collectives and in more conventionally managed Law Centres. A member of staff in one Law Centre explained that the previous financial year there had been "a 10% cut in salary so we could keep afloat, so that's how we've managed to get by". A 15% cut was under consideration in another Law Centre. In yet another Law Centre a staff member described how the collective had taken the decision to take a voluntary pay cut, a decision that she had found very difficult, knowing as she did that some staff members would find it particularly hard to cope on the reduced salary, given their family responsibilities.

"It's extremely difficult ... it's not something you do lightly", she reflected, pointing out that the staff were not keen to "undermine our own employment rights". She drew parallels with the situations that affected other public service workers. Public service professionals such as nurses were often depicted as "angels", but this was unhelpful, potentially trading upon their commitment, in her view. But "they still have to pay the rent".

Arrangements for holidays and time off in lieu had also come under consideration. In one Law Centre, for example, staff had been working very long hours in order to cope with the volume of work, and apparently amassing considerable amounts of time off in lieu. This had been an issue that the management committee had decided to address.

Long working hours without compensation in time off in lieu were widespread, it emerged. For some staff, this was simply what they did in order to meet the demand for services. "We work harder, we do more work in our own time in the evenings", explained a lawyer in one Law Centre. But this was a problematic strategy, it was argued by others, when the result was staff time off for sickness and staff burn-out. For some, the pressures became untenable, leading to decisions to leave, despite their overall commitment to working for access to justice for all. The issues of long working hours and unpaid overtime are more fully explored in Chapter Eight, which addresses the dilemmas associated with such labours of love both for paid staff and for volunteers.

Use of volunteers

In addition to developing more effective ways of organising the work, some Law Centres were evidently finding ways of coping that included increasing the use of volunteers and/or using volunteers more effectively. Volunteers could help out with administrative work, for instance, and provide cover for reception work, as well as providing casework support if they had relevant background knowledge and experience (such as law students and recently qualified lawyers). There were, in addition, examples of very experienced lawyers providing pro bono advice at Law Centres, sometimes over many years.

As one respondent suggested, volunteers fell into different categories. There were those volunteers who had recently completed a law qualification and were keen to obtain experience. They generally wanted legal rather than administrative experience and tended not to stay very long (which posed its own challenges for Law Centres in terms of continuity of service provision). As employment opportunities had been becoming more restricted, the use of volunteer lawyers was described as beginning to raise additional issues. Such volunteering opportunities could be described as unpaid internships.

This posed dilemmas in that it was widely argued that unpaid internships were potentially exploitative and that people should be paid the rate for the job. As a trade unionist involved with Law Centres reflected, Law Centres had always relied on volunteers, but "increasingly it's going to be exploitation of volunteers", and in the current situation "I've got no doubt they will be using unemployed solicitors, who want to keep their hand in, which will be total exploitation of those individuals and not fair for them either". "It's just the government getting any kind of legal advice or legal support on the cheap, basically", he concluded.

Despite reservations about the notion of unpaid internships, however, Law Centres could be faced with increasing pressures to provide such opportunities, raising additional questions about how to allocate them fairly, in line with equalities considerations (an issue upon which the Law Centres Federation (LCF) was providing guidance). One suggestion was that preference might be given to those from local communities, young people without family connections in the legal profession who might find it even more difficult to find a route into the profession than those from more privileged backgrounds.

Overall, the economic downturn had meant that it was easier to find good volunteers, and there was increasing evidence of competition for volunteering opportunities. A recently qualified volunteer in a Law Centre reflected in comparable vein: "I want to repeat that it is really difficult to get into volunteering. Most of my friends say that it is really difficult because people expect you to have this experience but how are you supposed to have this experience while you are applying for a volunteering position? ... it is really difficult." Volunteers were very aware of the benefits of obtaining such experience, however, and contrasted the benefits of volunteering in a Law Centre, which provided induction and training, with the experience of volunteering elsewhere. One young volunteer reflected that in the (private) firm of solicitors where he had previously volunteered, "they don't train you, they don't induct you – you make the coffee and tea".

In addition, there were volunteers who were students working for and completing other qualifications, such as administrative qualifications. Some of these were described as being "fantastic", while others were described as being more trouble to supervise than they were worth, in terms of their contribution. "Some volunteer because they really mean it", it was suggested, "but some volunteer to fill a gap", although it was also pointed out that volunteers often changed their views through their experiences of volunteering in the Law Centre and coming to appreciate its ethos.

There were also volunteers who provided very particular skills, such as fundraising, for example. Here again, this was sometimes because they were unable to find paid employment utilising their specific skills; one long-term volunteer fundraiser explained, for example, that she was unable to find a suitable job despite having a master's degree in business administration. She had hoped that gaining experience as a volunteer would assist in finding paid work, but this had so far failed to materialise. "I would love to have a [paid] job", she concluded, however much she enjoyed volunteering at the Law Centre.

These types of volunteer (with particular skills and experience, developed over a number of years) tended to stay for longer than did younger people embarking on their careers, it was suggested – with potentially greater value for Law Centres, which needed relatively long-term commitment. There were instances of Law

Centres requiring volunteers to commit to three- or even six-month periods, in order to maximise the benefits of unpaid labour, for example. Volunteers take time and energy to organise and support, if they are to contribute effectively, a point that was emphasised across the board by Law Centre staff, colleagues from other agencies and lawyers in private practice. Unless they stayed for some time, the benefits might be limited. The benefits of volunteering have to be reciprocal, it was argued.

It was also suggested that, with time and resources, more could be achieved through providing training opportunities for students. Some Law Centres had on-going relationships with legal training agencies. A lawyer with extensive experience of both Law Centres and legal training pointed out that this was very important for two reasons: providing services to meet unmet need in the short term, and also motivating law students to undertake pro bono work in their future careers. Initially, the newer universities had been predominant in this field. Now, however, the older universities were engaging too (maybe partly as a result of wider pressures to include some reference to corporate social responsibility in their mission statements). There may also have been pressures from students, in terms of wanting to strengthen their CVs and so improve their future employability. If all law schools provided this and reached even 50 clients a year, it could still make a significant contribution towards addressing unmet need, it was suggested, as well as having the potential to make major impacts on policy.

While this same lawyer/academic was enthusiastic about what could be achieved, he also emphasised the importance of being realistic about the limitations. Universities had to focus upon the educational aspects. So, for example, they would not necessarily take on cases if similar cases had already been explored by the students in question. There were also limits to the cases that could be taken on, in terms of their complexity. There was no way in which this type of university initiative could substitute for the provision of legal aid advice more generally, then, although there could be important benefits, including the promotion of pro bono contributions to Law Centres in the future.

Meanwhile, as has already been suggested, in some areas experienced lawyers were providing regular advice sessions on a pro bono basis, contributing specialist knowledge and skills. But this was not the case everywhere (with geographical differences impacting upon the availability of potential professional volunteers). And even where lawyers were providing advice on a voluntary basis, this was generally only one aspect of the service (that is, providing advice but not being available to follow this up, necessarily). In addition, lawyers generally emphasised the importance of staying strictly within their own particular areas of specialist expertise, as the law had become increasingly complex and subject to rapid change. A property specialist might give advice on housing matters at an evening advice session, just as an employment lawyer might advise employees. But there were limits. Reflecting on a comment (made by another interviewee) that lawyers with specialist knowledge of shipping law were volunteering in a local Law Centre, a lawyer responded by describing this an "urban myth". This simply wouldn't happen, in his view.

In summary, it seemed clear that volunteers could make significant and potentially increasing contributions to the work of Law Centres and that this could be mutually beneficial, helping to perpetuate Law Centres' ethos and mission in future generations. But there was no way that volunteers – whether legally qualified or not – would be able to substitute for paid staff, for the future. Furthermore, volunteers are not cost free: they require support and training. There are parallels here with attempts to increase the use of volunteers in third sector organisations more generally, with similar dilemmas about the uses and potential abuses of volunteers and unpaid internships, where they may be substituting for the employment of paid staff. Chapter Eight takes up some of these issues more fully.

The use of telephone and internet-based mechanisms for delivering legal advice

One further strategy to address the pressures on Law Centres related to the use of telephone and internet delivery systems. The LSC was interested in promoting this as a means of increasing the cost-effectiveness of service provision, and so were a number of local authorities, for similar reasons. It has also been an issue of potential interest to Law Centres themselves, both in Britain and more widely.

In several areas there were joint electronic referral systems. This type of system was described as being "very successful" in one area, contributing to joined-up advice services in the city. A person accessing any one agency was effectively accessing all the advice services as s/he could be referred on to an appropriate agency if this was deemed necessary. It was also pointed out that electronic systems could strengthen the contributions being made by lawyers providing pro bono advice (facilitating more effective follow-ups).

Here too, though, there were limits to the strategy as a potential means to meet the needs of Law Centre clients. A local authority officer who had considered this reflected that while there was indeed scope for a telephone gateway system in the area, it was important to acknowledge that when it came to the actual advice needed, there were clients who "do really want to see a real person" face-to-face. There were a number of reasons for this, including the difficulties that clients with English as a second language might experience, especially if they had to use pay phones to make contact. Telephone gateways and internet access might work very well for some clients, but clients with complex problems and needs (including mental health issues) would continue to need face-to-face contact right from the start.

Management committees/boards of trustees

As previous chapters have already indicated, the administrative requirements related to the fixed fee system and the LSC's targets were also in some cases impacting upon the roles and compositions of management committees/boards of trustees.[1]

While some management committees/boards of trustees still retained community and user community representatives, others were less rooted in these ways. This was partly due to changes in the nature of communities and community organisations, it was suggested (with fewer powerfully organised tenants' federations and **trades councils** than had been the case in the past, for instance).

But it was also due to the time pressures that were involved, together with the demands for more specialist expertise, particularly legal and financial expertise. In some cases management committee members/trustees were being approached on the basis of the particular skill sets that they could bring, including experience of management elsewhere in the public sector and/or in private practice. While this was seen as a necessary response, there were concerns about the potential loss of more community-based representation. "It is a challenge to keep the community base while bringing in the expertise that we need", as the community worker in one Law Centre summarised this particular dilemma.

Management committees/trustees also spoke of some of the challenges that they had faced, including the challenges involved in decisions about making members of staff redundant and revisiting conditions of employment in Law Centres facing financial crises. An understanding of employment law, in addition to the requirements for other forms of management expertise, was key here. Somewhat ironically, a trade union background emerged as an example of particularly relevant expertise, in terms of providing the knowledge and experience to ensure that procedures were fair and that employees' rights were respected. It was "such a horrible position to get into". But "my job [as a management committee member] is to get the best for the organisation while being fair to the people we employ", one trade unionist reflected – although he added that "fairness is a relative concept. From a manager's point of view it is perfectly fair to make people redundant if you need to [in order to save the Law Centre] but employees obviously have a different view about what is fair."

Charging clients

As has also been suggested in previous chapters, the issue of whether to charge clients for services emerged as particularly contentious, being seen by some as the ultimate capitulation to market forces. For others, however, this was recognised as a perhaps necessary concession as part of the strategies to preserve Law Centre services in an increasingly challenging climate. One lawyer explained, for instance, that at this stage it might be necessary to explore the case for making modest charges in some areas if this was the only way to ensure access to justice. He pointed out that any form of charging was potentially problematic, however, risking undermining the Law Centre's ethos (of open access to justice, regardless of the ability to pay). Housing and benefits clients would be unlikely to be in a position to pay, in any case, although there might be some scope for charging for some immigration work, his colleague added, reflecting that she was "open to anything, to be honest", including setting up a separate trading arm if this was the only way to "keep going for my clients". In her view this would be a matter for the Law Centres as a movement, however, rather than for any one Law Centre. And she recognised that some people did have very strong objections to some such proposals that were currently under consideration within the Law Centres movement. Between them, these two lawyers summarised the range of views that were prevalent at this period.

Among those most opposed to charging it was argued that "all the staff and all the management committee members are really opposed" because "the ethos of the Law Centre would be undermined". Such a move would also put enormous administrative burdens on the staff, as they would have to deal with a range of issues such as VAT, for example, and it would be "running a business ... not providing for the community", it was argued. "Is the price too big?" the same Law Centre worker asked, to which he answered a clear "Yes". For a lawyer working in another Law Centre this was similarly an issue of principle, potentially "a resigning issue".

However, views were shifting as time went by, an administrator in one Law Centre reflected. Although the issue was deeply contentious it was definitely on the agenda and becoming less hypothetical as the threats to the availability of legal aid increased. Charging would be challenging to implement fairly, however, and would require new structures, such as the establishment of separate trading arms.

The potential viability of charging was similarly questioned by other stakeholders. The chief executive of a partner agency commented, "What makes them think that they'll make money?" What would they do if clients were unable to pay? "It's not the panacea that people may think, although it may help", he added. It might be more realistic, in his view, to set up a separate trading arm to take different types of cases, if Law Centres were able to compete effectively with private firms in their areas on both quality and price. As it was, funding from the LSC was failing to cover the real costs of providing the service. But how many Law Centre clients would be in a position to pay more than this, he wondered.

This point was similarly emphasised by a lawyer in private practice. Although he was absolutely not opposed in principle to charging, he questioned what kind of contribution clients on welfare benefits would actually be able to make. The level of funds received through charging would be "chicken feed", in his view, and the bookkeeping involved in levying such charges would be "madness", as well as potentially impacting upon the relationships between Law Centres and their clients in disadvantaged communities.

Finally, a lawyer in private practice who provided pro bono advice sessions in a local Law Centre reflected that if the Law Centre were to start charging clients, this might impact on her willingness to give her time voluntarily. "It [charging] wouldn't feel quite right." Charging would also raise administrative issues such as in relation to insurance, for instance. Nor did she consider that setting up a separate trading arm to cross-subsidise Law Centres' legal aid-type work would be a realistic option. Many private firms, such as the one in which she worked, were already effectively cross-subsidising legal aid work, in the sense that this was less profitable than their work in other areas of law. "Would I want to give my time if it was being charged for – I don't think I would", she concluded.

So charging had been a hotly debated issue. As one lawyer explained, for some of his colleagues in Law Centres this was "a slippery slope thing and if you tamper with that not only do you lose your own integrity, but the public you serve will start to see you as a money-making thing and not a community service. On the whole I agree with that." But, as he then went on to explain, "because I am not a purist, because I am a compromiser and an acknowledger of complexity I don't think you can simply leave it at that. If the consequence of leaving it at that is that you die and end up with no service I would say 'hang on that is an awful price to pay for simplicity and purity'." As he then added, however, charging was in some ways a "completely non answer", in any case, given the target clientele's restricted ability to pay.

Over time, there was evidently greater acceptance across Law Centres that whatever the problems, charging would need to be considered as part of any future survival strategy. This chimed with the more general views expressed by a trustee with wide-ranging experience of management in the public service sector, views that have already been quoted in Chapter Four. In her opinion, public policy reforms had been chiselling away at the public service ethos over past decades. Public attitudes could be softened up to accept changes, she suggested, and lines that had been thought to be firmly drawn could turn out to be lines drawn in the sand.

In summary, pressures to become more business-like were resulting in significant changes in the ways in which Law Centres were working, posing increasing dilemmas as Centres attempted to hold on to their ethos and values. Some Law Centres were finding ways to safeguard collaborative ways of working while meeting the administrative requirements of the LSC, just as some Law Centres were developing effective partnerships to provide more holistic services to clients, despite the pressures to compete with other providers, as Chapter Six describes in more detail. While there was continuing resistance to the processes of marketisation, the ground was shifting, as the discussion of attitudes towards charging has illustrated.

Note

[1] The name varied, depending upon the particular arrangements in different Law Centres, the term 'trustee' generally being applied to management committee members who also had responsibilities as trustees of Law Centres with the formal status of a charitable body.

SIX

Conflict and competition versus collaboration and planning

This chapter explores the pressures of increasing conflict and competition, on the one hand, as against the challenges involved in promoting collaboration and planning, on the other hand. The first section summarises the tendencies towards conflict and competition that had impacted on Law Centres' relationships with other agencies in the past. This sets the context for the discussion of public service modernisation, with its associated pressures towards increasing competition in more recent times – despite New Labour's attempts to promote partnership working in parallel. The final section explores the countervailing strategies that have been developed in a number of Law Centres, where the approach has been to build collaborative relationships, with joint planning in order to deliver more joined-up services aiming to meet clients' needs more holistically as well as more cost-effectively. This final section includes illustrations from case studies of collaborative strategies, as were being developed in particular Law Centres such as Avon and Bristol, Coventry and Nottingham, for example.

Pressures to collaborate or to compete

With public service modernisation creating increasingly competitive environments, there have been inherent tensions for many third sector organisations which have been required to compete for contracts, but also to collaborate, working with partners to provide services most cost-effectively. As previous chapters have already pointed out, public service modernisation agendas shifted under the New Labour government, with less emphasis upon privatisation and competition per se and increasing emphasis upon the importance of developing cross-sectoral partnerships (although competition was still a significant feature) (Newman and Clarke, 2009). As Alan Milburn has already been quoted as concluding, such partnerships were to be 'the cornerstone of the Government's modernisation programme in Britain', 'central to our drive to modernise key public services' (Milburn, 2001, p 33).

There were competing pressures, then, as third sector organisations struggled to survive in an increasing competitive climate. Partnership working was being promoted as a strategy for survival, but partnership working also entailed potential risks, and particularly so when there were significant power imbalances between the different partners involved (Balloch and Taylor, 2001; Glendinning et al, 2002). Smaller organisations, such as Law Centres, tended to feel particularly vulnerable, fearful of being swamped by more powerful partners, afraid that partnerships (particularly partnerships involving the private sector) would undermine their distinctive ethos.

Critics argued more generally that the shift from grant funding to contractual funding could 'be interpreted as a technology for exerting power over the voluntary sector' (Buckingham, 2009, p 235), promoting increasing marketisation as the prerequisite for success in bidding for contracts as part of such partnerships. There was a paradox here, Buckingham (among others) continued, given that increasingly competitive markets had been shown to erode the 'open communication and collaboration that had previously been integral to their [voluntary sector organisations'] work' (Buckingham, 2009, p 248).

The notion of competition and collaboration as binary opposites belied the real complexity of the situation, and third sector organisations found themselves both competing and being encouraged to collaborate, while recognising that collaboration might turn out to be tokenistic or worse, undermining the weaker partners' distinctive identities and values along the line. The reality was shifting and complex for the voluntary sector, and especially so for smaller organisations such as Law Centres.

Given their roles of challenging service providers on behalf of their clients on the one hand, while engaging in preventative policy work (often with the very same service providers) on the other, Law Centres' relationships with these agencies were already complex and frequently characterised by elements of both collaboration and competition. And this was even before the advent of public service modernisation agendas. As Williams (2006, p 2) points out more generally, 'Competition and collaboration are integrally linked – two sides of a coin, though the contentious side for VCOs [voluntary and community organisations] is competition'. This was inevitably so, perhaps, with Law Centres, given their role as advocates, enabling their clients to pursue their rights and challenge unfair or inequitable treatment. Although a number of Law Centre staff commented on the relatively collaborative relationships that they had developed with public officials such as local authority officers, for example, they also recognised that these relationships could become strained. Lawyers could find themselves cross-examining officers in court one day and then speaking to them on the telephone the next, seeking collaboration on another issue. Such potential tensions were inherent in their roles.

A management committee member from a Law Centre reflected as follows on these paradoxes in the Centre's relationships with other agencies (including the NHS, for example). There was sympathetic understanding of the ways in which organisations such as the NHS were experiencing their own funding challenges, which impacted on their abilities to meet clients' needs. Hospitals were under pressure to move patients on, for instance, whether or not there was adequate provision for care in the community. But it was important that such understanding should not prevent the Law Centre from pursuing clients' rights and entitlements effectively. A staff member from another Law Centre commented in parallel that, while understanding the pressures that colleagues in other agencies and services were experiencing, "it was important not to let this go too far, or you could end up colluding in a situation in which the client wasn't getting what they needed" (such as getting their housing repairs done, for instance). Sometimes agencies did have to be challenged, she concluded, whatever the pressures on them.

In some areas it was clear that local authorities had uncooperative attitudes towards their local Law Centre, in any case, and no intention of providing resources, let alone collaborating. Such relationships were inevitably more conflictual, although here too, in practice, there were sometimes complexities and ambiguities. A staff member explained that the Law Centre in question had collaborative relationships with particular local authority officers, despite the fact that the councillors, in contrast, tended to see the Law Centre as "a thorn in their side". "A pain in the arse" was how a lawyer in another Law Centre described local councillors' view of the Centre. Even in this particular locality, though, relationships with some officers remained generally positive, despite sporadic conflicts of interest with policy makers.

There were also examples of situations in which a change of political control following a local election had led to the breakdown of previously relatively constructive relationships (although, in more than one case, a subsequent change of political control had later reversed this situation). These relationships were potentially fragile, then, and were expected to become even more fragile with the impact of public service modernisation agendas, compounded by the next round of public expenditure cuts, which were widely expected to impact on local authority funding in the next financial year.

The impact of public service modernisation: an increasingly competitive context

As previous chapters have already pointed out, one of the distinctive features of public service modernisation agendas, and of marketisation agendas more generally, has been the pressure to compete (despite parallel pressures from New Labour to collaborate), competition being assumed to promote increasing efficiency and choice. Many Law Centres had already had some experience of competing with other agencies, such as the CABs. But the funding system for legal aid that was introduced following the Carter reforms exacerbated previously existing tendencies towards competition as agencies bid against each other for contracts.

The result could be staff mistrust between different agencies, especially in cases where the larger advice agencies were seen as "predatory" when it came to bidding for contracts. Other studies have identified similar widespread fears that the contracting culture generally favoured larger VCOs (Milbourne, 2009) while adding to the pressure on smaller ones.

Pressures to compete were being compounded by fears about how legal and advice services would be funded (or not) in the future – described as a literal "fight for survival". A newly appointed Law Centre worker explained, for example, that when he had joined the staff the focus had been on the LSC tender, a bidding process in which the Law Centre had been successful. But the bidding process had involved competition between different agencies, which he described as having been a "kill or be killed situation". One agency a few miles away was actually going out of business as a result of losing out in this bidding process, while a couple of other advice centres had closed in recent years, he said. He reflected that he had been shocked by the competitive element, and concluded that, in his view, this was not in the best interests of providing a holistic service in the area.

This example illustrates Milbourne's premise that 'Competitive funding and performance frameworks embedded in local area commissioning undermine collaboration and constrain innovative, front-line work, the very work for which community-based organisations have gained positive reputations for addressing social problems' (Milbourne, 2009). There were disparities here between political agendas that recognised the value of the voluntary sector, on the one hand, and, on the other hand, funding systems that were apparently undermining their unique value;– their ability to engage and work with diverse and disadvantaged communities (Milbourne, 2009).

A number of those involved with Law Centres commented that the problem was not only that the LSC funding system was not funding collaborative ways of working. The system "actually drives wedges between organisations that should be working together". This view contrasted sharply with the LSC's given objectives for community legal aid, which stressed greater collaboration (including the promotion of greater collaboration via the LSC's proposals for CLACs and CLANs). As another of those involved with Law Centres reflected, the reality was that there were "potential tensions with other advice agencies" inherent in the bidding process itself. So far, relationships had actually remained positive in that particular area, "but pressures have been increasing, potentially leading to more tensions in future".

A stakeholder from an advice agency commented, in a somewhat more positive vein on the on-going tensions between collaboration and competition, recognising the potential for collaboration and partnership, as well as the pressures towards increasing competition:

> "There will be opportunities where we can work together and there may also be times when we are 'a bit pissed off' when the other is delivering something that you wanted to, but after a few days you are back to working together again. There is a lot of trust there but it's a complex relationship and also quite healthy that we don't trust each other completely. It keeps us on our toes."

Collaboration could be advantageous, then, despite the countervailing pressures. Where Law Centres and other advice services had already formed partnerships, bidding processes were experienced less negatively, in that the partners had positioned themselves in ways that made them externally more competitive, being able to make collective decisions about sharing resources and developing coordinated approaches to service provision.

Conflicting pressures

While there was evidence that Law Centres were experiencing increasing pressures towards competition, the reality was more complex. There were also pressures towards increasing partnership working and greater collaboration. These pressures emanated from the top down, not only from New Labour's approach to public service modernisation in general and the LSC's approach more specifically, but also from other agencies, particularly local authorities, seeking to develop more strategic (and more cost-effective) services in their areas.

But more collaborative approaches also emanated from the bottom up as Law Centres and other agencies developed joint strategies based upon partnership working. In an examination of the varying responses to the conflicting pressures both to compete and to collaborate, experiences can be plotted across a wide spectrum. Even where there were examples of successful collaborative partnerships, stakeholders also recognised the pressures, and sometimes the necessity, of competition. As a CAB director reflected: "One of the challenges is – when are we partners and when are we competing?" In his view, while the CAB and the Law Centre were "natural allies" and working closely within an advice network, occasions had arisen when only one advice partner was needed in bidding for a particular funding opportunity. He added that "as our relationship matures" they would have to find a way to manage this tension.

There were other examples of this kind of complexity in practice. For example, one Law Centre mentioned its involvement in capacity building and the provision of specialist support to other advice agencies, such as CABs. However, this was deemed problematic by others in the area, as some CABs saw themselves as being in potential competition rather than in collaboration with the Law Centre in question.

The LSC's own interventions to promote collaboration and the development of consortia were a relevant factor in this shifting policy context. As was pointed out in Chapter Two, the LSC had aimed to promote joint bidding, through the development of CLACs and CLANs. The piloting of CLACs and CLANs had provided evidence of the challenges inherent in this type of top-down approach, however, as Chapter Two has also illustrated.

In one area, for example, attempts to develop a CLAC had ultimately led to less rather than more collaboration. This was despite a positive starting point. A group of agencies had been working with the local authority in this particular area, aiming to develop an advice partnership in order to provide a more holistic service and improve referrals for clients. The main reasons given for the situation's implosion were that there had been insufficient time or resources to build partners' relationships and this had undermined previously existing levels of trust, with smaller agencies having concerns about being "swallowed up" by larger providers.

As Kail and Abercrombie have argued in relation to collaboration in the voluntary sector more widely, successful collaborations require an investment of time and money if they are to be effective (Kail and Abercrombie, 2013). In this case, the problems associated with the lack of time and resources were further exacerbated by uncertainties about funding, together with uncertainties about the future of CLACs themselves.

In summary, many of those involved expressed severe misgivings about the impact of the Carter changes for Law Centres in terms of the effects on increasing competition – despite the LSC's somewhat unsuccessful attempts to promote collaboration via the CLACs and CLANs. It was suggested that the push to become more managerial, entrepreneurial and ultimately more "business-like" was not only in danger of radically changing the rationale of Law Centres. This was also "fracturing the Law Centres movement".

The failures of the CLACs and Clans raise further questions about what conditions would needed in order to foster effective collaborative working. Was this an approach that could be imposed, particularly in a climate of cuts? Or would that be counterproductive? The effects of cuts, combined with the pressures associated with public service modernisation more generally, were being seen as undermining previous relationships of trust and the advice sector's ability to respond collaboratively to identifiable needs.

Alternative approaches: partnerships responsive to community needs developed from the bottom up

There were examples of alternative approaches, however, where there was active resistance to increasing competition from the bottom up, starting from the recognition that different agencies had different areas of expertise – which could be shared for mutual benefit. Collectively, it was argued, they could best meet the needs of the groups and communities that they aimed to serve and collectively they stood the best chance of survival. Law Centres were frequently cited as being a fundamental and irreplaceable part of such wider advice networks, providing a cornerstone of expert legal advice and recourse to justice. That these types of strategies differed from the LSC's approach was explained as follows: "We see a broad range of services meeting the different need of different communities as inherently a good thing", and "We don't think that centralisation is necessarily a good thing when it comes to advice services".

In other words, partnerships needed to start from responses to local needs. This was contrasted with partnerships starting from the needs of the market – how to succeed in winning bids on commercial criteria. Large national organisations could offer economies of scale, winning contracts by undercutting smaller providers. But large national providers would lack the local networks and the locally rooted understandings that enabled smaller, more locally based organisations to meet community needs more effectively, it was argued.

In one particular instance the agencies in question chose to promote a "stand together – die alone kind of approach". In doing so, city-wide they brought together both the (relatively) larger advice agencies (including the Law Centre) and the smaller, community-based agencies to form a network that collectively gathered data and mapped access to advice geographically. They worked closely with the local authority to help to develop the most effective allocation of resources and to ensure that provision was responsive to identified areas of need. This approach clearly also had potential implications for greater efficiencies and savings, maximising cost-effectiveness. This example also highlights the scope for building common ground between local policy makers and third sector organisations where there were shared commitments to providing responsive, 'joined-up' local services.

These types of partnership from the bottom up seemed to offer win-win solutions. Still, there were challenges inherent in such approaches– even where there were already strong collaborative partnerships. One Law Centre worker reflected, when describing a newly promoted consortium with the CAB and other agencies, that this approach was "totally new to us. It could be a good thing. But it could also cause tensions." These challenges needed to be addressed.

In the areas that offered examples of the most effective partnerships, staff and stakeholders tended to express feelings of improved morale and more positive outlooks on their ability to contend with current challenges. For example, as one of those involved explained, funding issues represented "a huge challenge. I think the Legal Aid cuts are going to decimate huge sections of the country", but in their city the advice agencies had worked collectively with the local authority and secured core funding which, he believed, would allow them to survive the next three years at least.

Conversely, in an area where there had been significant competitive pressures the consequent breakdown of collaborative networks had impacted negatively on staff within the Law Centre as well as across the advice sector more generally. One of those involved concluded that he would "love to have been able to describe the situation in terms of the 'Dunkirk spirit'", all pulling together in the face of external challenges. But this hadn't actually been the case. On the contrary, the pressures had led to internal divisions. There was "a lack of solidarity", and more mutual suspicion, both within the Law Centre and within the advice sector more widely.

Key drivers for collaboration, despite the challenges

Genuine and effective collaboration has been notoriously difficult to achieve, especially when this has involved collaborating cross-sectorally. As Williams has reflected, 'alliances require commitment, flexibility and a willingness to share control' (Williams, 2006, p 26), and with 'clearly defined goals so that all the partners can focus on an ultimate purpose'. Research into successful collaborative models has also highlighted the need for those involved to work on the processes required to develop such partnerships in the first place, as well as working on the formal structural arrangements entailed (Flynn, 2007). As Milbourne and Cushman's research has similarly concluded, 'cross-sector trust can be generated and sustained in situations where time and effort are jointly invested in understanding and learning from different approaches. However, this demands significant investment in communication and co-creating purposes, meanings and values in the project. It also demands the kinds of projects and infrastructural investment which are currently being eroded' (Milbourne and Cushman, 2013, p 504). This finding was confirmed by the experiences of a number of Law Centres.

Staff commented on the time and the resources that were needed to develop collaborative partnership work. But the output-oriented funding system was signally failing to provide for this. Networking with other agencies, groups and community organisations had "gone" because this "takes time" and was not funded. As a result, one Law Centre had become more isolated within its locality. The situation had then been exacerbated by the process of competing for contracts, a process which, it was argued, was undermining networking and cohesion across the advice sector more generally.

This was reiterated in an area where, historically, the Law Centre had worked with other local organisations in order to reach specific groups, working through the local Women's Advice Centre, for example, to reach a range of women in the area. Law Centre staff explained that they would "have to cut back [on this outreach work] because we don't get paid by anybody for the time spent going there". This Law Centre had also been involved in a local forum of advice agencies, including the CAB and a refugee centre. The forum was "struggling to continue strictly because the time taken by any of us going to a meeting there which may take three hours including travelling, this time we should be spending on worrying about our own agencies and our own businesses and trying to keep them going".

Despite these challenges, there were examples of Law Centres that were still developing collaborative ways of working, building partnerships in order to meet community needs most effectively, and identifying resources to enable them to build such partnerships in the first place. Their reasons for doing this – the benefits of collaboration – were cited (in no particular order) as follows:

- sharing resources, and thereby using resources most cost-effectively
- sharing expertise, and effectively building capacity in the process
- improving the ability to formulate stronger projects and to bid for funding for these more effectively
- developing more effective systems for cross-referral
- consolidating data, creating fuller evidence on local needs and on the take-up of services within the area
- improving staff morale as a result of not feeling so isolated

- strengthening strategic responsiveness, rather than remaining trapped in reactive 'fire-fighting' and, most importantly,
- resulting in better, more holistic services for the clients.

These resonate with research findings on the reasons for developing collaborative relationships within the voluntary sector more widely. For example, Williams (2006) summarised the advantages of developing alliances as the abilities to:

- achieve strategic synergy
- increase the speed of operations
- share risks
- share resources, technology and management systems and
- increase the range and scale of activities through increased abilities to secure new contracts.

The role of local authorities in promoting collaboration

In response to both the competitive funding environment and the need for greater efficiency, Stuffins (2011) has suggested that 'more unusual or innovative collaborations could be encouraged by local authorities. With their own over-arching view of the voluntary sector in their area, councils are uniquely placed to help facilitate these partnerships'.

The role of local authorities and their approach to the advice sector emerged as significant factors in the case study areas' resilience in contending with current challenges. In a number of areas the local authority was viewed as being directly responsible for whether competition or collaboration between agencies was the pervading influence. For example, a councillor in one case study area reflected that "we've always believed in partnership" and therefore had a strong commitment to this. The Law Centre was pivotal in this approach to ensuring that the most disadvantaged could have "access to legal remedies and some sort of justice". The councillor described the then current situation as "the most challenging circumstances we've ever been in", and concluded that there was consequently a distinct need "to pull together and support each other".

In another city an advice agency representative described the local authority's approach to commissioning advice services in similar terms. He explained that "There is understanding that there is a better way to commission than straightforwardly competitive tendering and that it's important to take a more strategic approach to advice services as a whole in the city." This had enabled and supported the agencies in their efforts to "make things work better with clear pathways that all of the agencies use". This was seen to provide a better service, ultimately, for those seeking advice at any single agency or point of contact. The impetus for this had partly come from the local authority in question, but there had also been a strong push from the agencies themselves; an attitude described as "let's do the best that we can with it" in the interests of the clients. One of the frequently cited motivations for collaboration was in fact precisely this last point – improving services and access to them for those most in need.

Coordinated bids for resources

Through collaborating, advice networks were succeeding in obtaining additional resources, as well as ensuring that existing resources were being used most effectively. In Nottingham, for example, Advice Nottingham obtained funding from the Big Lottery that enabled the umbrella organisation to develop its collaborative partnership. This, it was explained, "enabled us to come to the position we're in now" as a well-established consortium. Together with the council, it had identified gaps in provision, developing joined-up services to meet the needs of different areas and client groups. Having funding to build the consortium also enabled the organisations involved to be "ahead of the game" in terms of putting in other funding bids. It was planning to bid for additional resources to develop its website, for instance, using information technologies to provide a single reference point for clients covering all of the services provided by Advice Nottingham partners.

Advice Services Coventry had similarly obtained additional funding, in this case from Neighbourhood Renewal Funding as well as from the Big Lottery and the Baring Foundation. In total, Advice Services Coventry had already obtained almost £1,000,000. These funding resources enabled it to fund a coordinator to develop the partnership. It too had developed a joint electronic referral system that was described as being "very successful" in maximising the effectiveness of advice provision in Coventry. Like Nottingham, it had also developed joint training, another way of ensuring the most effective use of resources.

Advice Centres for Avon had also obtained funding from the Big Lottery and the Baring Foundation, enabling the organisation to fund three posts. These three staff members built relationships with funders, developing consortia bids as well as developing collaborative work more generally. Together, the Advice Centres built a library of resources relating to common policies and procedures, further contributing to the development of coordinated service provision so as to meet advice needs holistically.

Local authority staff themselves gave a number of reasons for working with existing providers to support a collaborative approach to the commissioning and provision of advice services. These overlapped to some considerable extent with advice agencies' own motivations and included the aims of:

- providing more joined-up services
- offering clients better coverage
- facilitating cross-referrals
- avoiding conflicts of interest
- targeting provision for specific groups
- sharing resources and expertise and deploying limited resources more effectively and
- supporting the voluntary sector more generally.

A genuine partnership approach would clearly require both leadership and buy-in from the agencies involved, as fully active partners. Law Centres were frequently regarded as lead or key partners in these types of networks and were appreciated as such for their core values and ethos. As an advice centre worker commented, reflecting on the role played by the local Law Centre manager, she had been "selfless in putting herself forward to represent all of them [the advice agencies involved in the partnership] and the work they do", rather than simply representing the interests of the Law Centre in question. "We'd be lost without them", reflected another stakeholder, recognising the importance of Law Centres' specialist expertise. Similar comments were made by local authority officers, concerning Law Centres' pivotal roles.

Local authority officers recognised that while there may sometimes be tensions (when Law Centres supported clients in making complaints against the local authority, for instance), Law Centres' independence had been vital. This was not only because Law Centres ensured access to justice for individuals and communities. It was also because they could contribute to policy development, leading to service improvements more widely. Some local authorities clearly valued these aspects of Law Centres' independent roles, despite the potential tensions that needed to be managed. A local authority officer reflected that a better exchange of information between the local authority and the Law Centre could actually lead to systems change, thereby reducing the problems that had led to complaints in the first place:

> "Where there is a tension is probably around the tackling discrimination service where you get cases that are against the council and actually what we would like is to have some anonymised information about the types of cases against the council so we can use that to learn from it and actually think about stopping things from happening rather than a number of cases going in and actually the legal challenge being taken all the way."

In several areas, the local authorities in question had either recently undertaken a strategic review or were in the process of doing so. In these instances the strategic reviews included concern to promote precisely such preventative approaches – as well as concerns, of course, about questions of efficiency and the most effective use of diminishing resources. In summary, these strategic reviews focused upon supporting collaboration between the different advice agencies within the local authority area and promoting greater integration, with clear definition of roles based on differing fields of expertise and different areas of geographical coverage. In one pertinent case, for example, a local authority representative explained that:

> "We have commissioned them to join up better and to think about strengths and not duplicate. They have thought more about where they deliver and who to and defined themselves or extended and

developed more. There are some natural geographic boundaries but they have had to look at joining up better."

This was underpinned by the local authority's commitment to the advice sector, ring-fencing funding and resisting what was seen as a premature "move to joint commissioning" via the LSC's promotion of CLACs and CLANs. The local authority's resistance had been due to its awareness of the needs of the network of advice provision and its desire to build capacity in the sector before the new commissioning approach was implemented. A local authority officer commented that "because we worked with the sector and the advice network and we went to consultation with the sector" it was a lengthy process, but one that had paid off in that "there has been a real change through this process", with the result that "it feels far more like a partnership now rather than us and them".

For a number of local authorities and advice sector agencies the ideal scenario was described as "customer focused", with the client having access to advice at any point across the advice network. The client would then be referred to the most appropriate agency, depending upon their individual needs. This type of advice network recognised the vital role of the Law Centre as the source of specialist legal advice and support, underpinning the advice services that were being offered across the rest of the network. In several instances where this type of joined-up service had developed there had been investment in setting up shared systems for monitoring and referring clients. This had additional benefits for the local authority and for the advice sector overall in that it was building a more comprehensive picture of the levels of service needs and service usage.

This all contrasted with areas where there had been a tendency for greater competition and less collaboration. In such areas, typically, there had been less-supportive relationships between Law Centres and their local authorities. These tensions had been exacerbated with the introduction of competitive tendering. As one Law Centre staff member described the situation:

"Competition has crept in; we're all competing for the same pot of money – a typical example is the CAB and the Law Centre competing for funding from the local authority and so the question is: whose bid is better? You have to make an assessment on whose bid is better and how much they get. Sometimes you split it down the middle and you say OK, half each. But in another situation there's just £10 on the table, only one person's going to get it so it's going to be winner takes it all. And it is going to be on the basis of a bid."

The consequences of a solely competitive approach driven by a scarcity of funding undermined the possibilities of an integrated advice sector providing complementary services. Instead, such an approach seemed likely to favour the survival of some agencies at the cost of others. This was precisely why some local authorities had opted for a more collaborative approach to commissioning advice services, aiming to develop more strategic approaches to meeting local needs.

Collaboration and planning from the bottom up

Bristol City Council was one among a number of local authorities that had developed strategic approaches to the provision of advice services in the area. Together with South Gloucestershire local authority it had been critical of the proposal for a CLAC pilot, arguing that such a top-down initiative would potentially cause "damage to community control and accountability". Instead, Bristol City Council worked with the Advice Network (Advice Centres for Avon) that had been established under the Law Centre's leadership to agree on joint measuring tools in order to build a comprehensive picture of advice needs and services across the city. This approach, building from existing networks, "seemed to work", in the local authority's view, providing the information that council officers needed in order to plan their commissioning and funding processes effectively to meet local needs.

This planning process was lengthy and difficult at times, as a council officer explained, and there had been "some friction". But the end result had been positive. This was a real partnership, rather than an "us and them" approach. Each provider had its own identity, "which is one of the things that makes it an interesting and vibrant sector", the officer concluded. Gaps in services for particular areas, such as areas in the east of the city, had been identified in the process. The commissioning process that followed took account of the need to address such gaps, along with the need to ensure clearer access points for clients more generally. The end result was that providers put in their separate bids in complementary ways, focusing on clients' needs. "I think the way forward is collaboration", one of the stakeholders concluded, reflecting on the process and the outcomes overall.

Similarly, when reviewing its strategy for providing advice services, Coventry City Council had consulted with Advice Services Coventry, a network of advice agencies that had been working together "to coordinate the delivery of advice services in the city" with the aim of providing "seamless service pathways for clients". Here too the Law Centre played a leading role, along with the CAB. The different agencies had developed ways of coordinating access for clients and clarifying referrals between generalist and specialist providers.

In Nottingham the local authority had decided to collaborate but "stay on the outside" as a partner with Advice Nottingham, the umbrella organisation that facilitated coordination between the Law Centre, the CAB, Shelter and other advice agencies in the area. These organisations had previously competed against each other for funding, before deciding to "get ahead of the game" by collaborating, developing a consortium rooted in their shared ethos and values. They worked closely with the local authority, aiming to create a joined-up service comprehensively meeting clients' needs. Here too, the Law Centre was fulfilling what other stakeholders described as a "tremendous role", providing leadership and specialist expertise.

Collaborating, competing with or becoming more like the private sector?

If partnership working with local authorities and other service providers was potentially challenging, collaborating with private sector firms was even more so. How to maintain Law Centres' distinctive ethos in the context of increasing marketisation? There had been pressures on Law Centres to become more business oriented in any case, as previous chapters have already argued.

For a number of critics (Buckingham, 2009; Milbourne, 2009), it was the pressure of the then current policy and funding regimes that was eroding the voluntary sector's autonomy and ethos, which were fundamental to its ability to deliver effective community-level services. As Buckingham has commented, 'Concerns have been raised about the erosion of the voluntary sector's autonomy, its capacity to campaign for social change and its ability to engage local communities' (Buckingham, 2009, p 235). This dilemma had been summed up in a report commissioned by the Institute for Voluntary Action Research which found that the impact of public service reform on voluntary sector organisations was that 'some organisations have been drawn by the availability of funding away from community development and community responsiveness towards delivery of public services and services designed externally rather than in direct response to local need ... in making this shift, their potential to act as agents of community change or as advocate for local people has been diminished' (Cairns et al, 2006, p 6).

The pressures to become more 'business-like' link to the more specific question of the nature of Law Centres' relationships with the private sector itself: were these relationships characterised by competition or collaboration? There were questions as to whether Law Centres either could or should compete with private firms of solicitors; competing "on the basis of price was a no-winner", it was argued, unless they were to accept poorer conditions of employment and lower wages, while reducing the time and attention given to clients. These issues have already been considered in more detail in Chapter Five.

By contrast, however, there were instances where Law Centres did actually develop collaborative relationships with private legal practices. For example, one Law Centre cited a number of connections with private firms, including referrals from them based upon the Law Centre's specific expertise in welfare law and employment law. Some of these firms also offered the Law Centre pro bono work, doing surgeries, for instance, as part of their commitment to social responsibility. There are parallels here with experiences in the voluntary sector more widely, as Harris (2010, p 3) has pointed out: 'many businesses are actually dependent on cooperation from the VS [voluntary sector] in order to implement their CSR [corporate social responsibility] policies. This raises questions about the implications of the relationships with business for VSOs [voluntary sector organisations] themselves', however. In the Law Centre examples there were situations in which this type of relationship could be considered mutually beneficial – as well as examples to the contrary, as previous chapters have already outlined.

There were evidently benefits for private firms when such arrangements enhanced their corporate image, at the same time enabling their staff to gain useful experience, with the added possibility of new clients being referred to them, as Chapter Eight considers in more detail. This type of experience was echoed by a stakeholder who, as both a local councillor and a solicitor, had a critical understanding of the motivations of both the private sector and Law Centres. He explained that he used to do a voluntary weekly session at an income rights centre (subsequently the local Law Centre) and was supported in this by the private firm for which he was then working. This relationship was seen to be mutually beneficial, making a useful contribution to the wider society and facilitating referrals between agencies. He felt that there was considerable good will and positive motivation within private practice overall. He himself had become a lawyer in order to be able to help people, and he stressed that some lawyers within the private sector were motivated by similar ideals to those that motivated Law Centre staff.

As previous chapters have suggested, however, this was far from representing the whole picture. This particular councillor–solicitor also commented that the Law Centre was filling a gap that was not compensated for by law firms doing legal aid work and added that while 15 years previously someone could walk into a private law firm and get legal aid and the advice they needed, this was no longer the case. His view was that "access to justice has become increasingly more difficult for many people" as a result of a "terribly bureaucratic system that is more interested in processes than outcomes". In his view, opportunities for future collaboration with private firms were inherently limited.

A Law Centre staff member who had previously worked in the private sector commented in similar vein that there were advantages to collaboration with private sector firms, but the limits also needed to be recognised. In her view, "there are some good things about working in the private sector ... because it's profit driven it has to be very very efficient", and "I think that Law Centres can learn from that". "Actually there are ways of doing things ... it's about taking the best [practice]" and applying this to Law Centres, she concluded.

She recognised that this was not a view that was necessarily shared with other Law Centres, however. "Historically it's been seen as a bit of a 'them and us' situation ... with some competition." She referred to fears among Law Centres about whether working more closely with private firms "might make them turn into one", eroding Law Centre values and ethos in the process.

Overall, despite the reservations of so many of those working in Law Centres, there were in fact a number of instances where there had been positive collaborations with private sector firms. For example, one Law Centre had a partnership with a private practice that involved solicitors giving advice on areas of law that the Law Centre didn't cover. It was explained that "It's a good and positive arrangement that benefits the community" and, on a reciprocal note, the work with the Law Centre was part of the firm's approach to social responsibility. In broader reflection on this, the conclusion was that Law Centres could also develop other partnerships and still keep their local roots. These were "difficult times", but this was also an "opportunity" and "an impetus to change". "You can't go on delivering services as we did in the 1980s", in any case, it was argued. "We do need to be optimistic about ourselves and our ability to meet the challenges of the 21st century."

In one city the Law Centre manager described how it had come to be in a delivery partnership with an established private firm of solicitors and a CAB. He explained that before the partnership was established they would have regarded each other as competitors and that "under normal circumstances we wouldn't have looked at each other". In this new and more challenging context, however, they could see the benefits of collaborative approaches. They each had areas of specialism, and for each there were areas where they were not in a position to provide services. But, between the three partners, they were able to provide the full range of services. So, for example, the Law Centre was delivering welfare benefits provision at the private solicitors' offices and the CAB offices and the CAB was providing debt advice at the Law Centre. The Law Ccentre manager commented, in conclusion, that "it's been a success: each of us provides a full service in each centre".

In providing the rationale for this particular partnership, the Law Centre manager explained that he had sought to identify the Law Centre's nearest competitors and had then proceeded to explore ways in which they could collaborate rather than compete with each other. Before the tendering process for the next round of services was completed, the three partners had signed a memorandum of agreement. Once they had won the contract for this next round of services, they had proceeded to develop a more formal partnership agreement and cooperated increasingly on a range of related issues. There was "additional value for us all", in the manager's view, with scope for developing further forms of collaboration in the future.

There are parallels here with findings from previous research. For some, the current challenges facing the voluntary sector generally, with a blurring of sectoral boundaries and practices, offered opportunities such as 'the disciplines of marketing and strategic management' (Williams, 2006, p 2). For others, in contrast, they raised new questions, including questions about the costs and benefits of inter-organisational relationships, how partnerships could combine sectoral competencies and, overall, whether new partnerships could effectively improve services (Entwistle and Martin, 2005) without undermining organisations' ethos in the process.

In summary, while there have been powerful pressures towards increasing competition among advice sector providers, this has been far from the whole story. Despite the tensions, complexities and challenges involved in developing partnerships – especially partnerships involving private sector firms – without losing sight of organisations' missions and ethos, there are examples of positive approaches, developing forms of collaboration as part of alternative ways forward. Together they illustrate proactive ways of coping and of developing strategically planned and democratically accountable services to meet clients' needs holistically in response to the challenges associated with increasing marketisation, rather than engaging in increasing conflict and competition.

SEVEN

Public service modernisation and time

Previous chapters have discussed key aspects of the Carter reforms and subsequent change, as they impacted upon Law Centres, their ethos, values and practices, as well as on the working conditions of Law Centre staff and volunteers. The central issue of this chapter relates to questions of time and, more specifically, to questions of how recent changes have changed both the quantitative and the qualitative nature of working time. So many of the tensions and dilemmas that were being experienced were described in relation to time, in terms of increasing time pressures, in terms of differing notions and understandings of time efficiency and in terms of how time was being valued and measured in the provision of legal advice.

This chapter sets out to show how the accountability system that was put into place with the fixed fee system narrowed the amount of working time to be spent per case, while failing to include funding for time spent on more holistic or preventative work. These transformations of working time may be conceptualised as a re-emergence of Taylorist principles of work, it will be argued, an approach based upon maximising managerial control over the organisation and timing of work processes from the top down, rather than aiming to engage the energies and creativity of the workforce from the bottom up (as in the development of workplace quality circles, for example, approaches that had been widely debated in previous decades). The following section summarises debates on the New Public Management and the sociology of work and time, providing the context for the subsequent discussion of time pressures, along with the discussion of time being wasted – and, conversely, of time being valued – in Law Centres.

New Public Management, neo-Taylorism and the new organisation of (working) time in the public services

As previous chapters have already argued, over recent decades policy makers in Britain have sought to increase the importation of market mechanisms into the administration of publicly funded organisations, including the administration of Law Centres. It was argued that greater competition, an explicit measurement of outputs and performance as well as more generally a stress on a private sector style of management practices would produce a higher degree of efficiency and reduce cost – the changes in governance associated with New Public Management and New Managerialism (Hood, 1991; Power, 1999; Newman, 2000; Newman and Clarke, 2009).

Since the mid to late 1980s these had become models for the administration of the public sphere in health services (Newman and Lawler, 2009; Schofield,

2009), in education (Brennan, 2009), in local government and in the caring professions (Newman et al,2008; Healy, 2009), as well as in the provision of public legal services (Sanderson and Sommerlad 2011; Sommerlad, 2001). As previous chapters have also pointed out, these approaches underwent changes under the New Labour governments (Newman, 2000; Newman and Clarke, 2009) and again, more recently, under the Coalition government's strategies for welfare reform. But there have been common threads too, with the increasing use of market mechanisms as a strategy for public service reform more generally.

As Felts and Jos (2000) have opined, these reforms can be understood in terms of a reorganisation of time. They suggest that 'reform efforts that emphasized goal setting and outcome measurement' (Felts and Jos, 2000, p 520) in terms of public administration practices have been accompanied by a shift of the idea of time in general, and more particularly in terms of the idea of futurity. The model of the bureaucratic organisation which embodied the notions of predictability and calculability of the future gave way to the idea of the flexible organisation whose future is open to constant change. New Public Management approaches, as Felts and Jos argue, can be viewed as a reflection of this shift in the understanding of time. The 'emphasis upon flexible organizations, measurable performance criteria (i.e. benchmarks, goals, objectives), and the shorter time horizons made possible by contracting out clearly shows a bias in how to think about time' (Felts and Jos, 2000, p 525).

Felts and Jos argued that there were also inherent tensions and contradictions, pointing out that many of the reforms 'served mostly symbolic and rhetorical purposes' (Felts and Jos, 2000, p 520), part of wider strategies to discipline employees, including public service professional employees, more effectively. As du Gay has similarly suggested, the reforms were being implemented in a wider climate of distrust of the efficiency of public or bureaucratic organisations and their staff more generally (du Gay, 2000).

Donaldson has argued, in parallel, that the 'narrow model of human behaviour' (Donaldson, 1990, p 371) associated with such suspicions characterises public service professionals as having the 'inherent propensity to shirk, to be opportunistic, to maximize his or her self-interest, to act with guile, and to behave in a way that constitutes a moral hazard' (Donaldson, 1990, p 372) and needing to be managed with stricter control mechanisms and more rigorous forms of output measurement.

The changes in the governance of publicly funded organisations have been considered in the context of the re-emergence of Taylorist managerial practices, reverting to approaches that had been the subject, in previous decades, of fundamental criticism, in the context of debates on less negative approaches to the management of human resources. Taylorism – named after Frederick W. Taylor – describes a type of management of work processes in which the organisation and timing of work tasks are no longer performed with the degrees of control that were previously exercised by workers themselves. In contrast, under Taylorism, managers aim to control, standardise and hence time work processes by splitting them into measurable units. This practice has sought to increase time and cost efficiency, reducing workers' autonomy over work processes and requiring only fragments of the skills that had been needed in craft production.

Taylor's ideas originated at the beginning of the 20th century, in a socio-economic context of rapid industrialisation, mechanisation and the rise of mass production. Pollitt uses the term 'neo-Taylorism' to consider the application of Taylorist approaches to public service modernisation in the UK in more recent years. He argues that neo-Taylorist characteristics are evident in the development of clear performance indicators to measure the achievement of targets while paying less attention to the complexities of workplace norms, beliefs and aspirations (Pollitt, 1990, p 56) of individuals working in an organisation. Neo-Taylorist managerial approaches also encompass an 'emphasis on economy and efficiency, to the relative neglect of other values' and 'there is the scantiness of attention' 'afforded to staff as people to be encouraged and developed rather than as work units to be incentivised and measured' (Pollitt, 1990, p 59). In terms of practices and values, neo-Taylorist approaches emphasise output, efficiency and economy, while 'other values – for example, fairness, justice, representation, or participation – were either off the agenda or were treated as constraints on the drive for higher productivity' (Pollitt, 1990, 138).

The emergence of neo-Taylorist managerial practices in the provision of public services has also been suggested in a more recent study by Stoney (2001). Drawing on empirical research on the changing managerial context in local authorities in the UK, Stoney claims that Taylorist principles continue to guide organisational values and practices. This is so in particular in regard to the absence of autonomy over the allocation of working time, the control of the content and timing of people's work as well as in regard to processes of work intensification. Pollitt similarly argues that one of the most important elements constituting neo-Taylorist managerial practics is a strong division between strategic objective-setting management, on the one hand, and front-line operational line management with few influences over the actual work process, on the other hand (Pollitt, 1990).

Crowley et al (2010) have similarly argued that neo-Taylorist managerial practices are not simply features of a bygone industrial era, as had been widely supposed – but had actually been reinstated with the advent of post-Fordist modes of production. Contrary to commonly assumed ideas that work under post-Fordist conditions radically departs from the Taylorist principles of time discipline,[1] standardisation and hierarchical organisations, Crowley et al suggest that 'principles of scientific management (…) have assumed key positions in the post-Fordist era' (Crowley et al, 2010, p 423). In other words, while post-Fordist modes of production have increased the need for flexibility in the production process as well as among the workforce, there has also been an expansion of control mechanisms, less time autonomy, a stronger focus on output measurement and an intensification of work processes for the worker – all being elements that characterise neo-Taylorist managerial practices.

Crowley et al argue that '[t]hese flexible practices, which reflect an expanded scope of Taylor's methods, have heightened performance pressure and impinged on the nature of professional work and employee well-being' (Crowley et al, 2010, p 441). While Crowley et al ground their empirical research in workplace ethnographies conducted between 1929 and 1999, there are more recent indications of a spread of neo–Taylorist practices, with significant effects on the organisation of working time in the provision of public services, including the provision of legal aid via Law Centres.

Importantly, in relation to questions of time, with the reforms that followed the Carter report, most areas of legal aid changed from a system based on hourly rates to a fixed fee system. As previous chapters have already explained, this fixed fee was calculated on the average amount of time considered necessary to finish cases in particular areas of law. The only variation was the provision for additional funding for exceptional cases – defined as cases requiring more than three times the value of the fixed fee for that particular area of law.

The underlying aim was that providers of legal advice should start to act in more business–like ways, balancing the cases that could require more time than the fixed fee provided for with a higher number of short cases that could be closed in less time. In summary, the fixed fee system incentivised Law Centres to spend less time per case, and to close cases in a timely way. This would generate surpluses that could then be used to offset the additional time taken by more complex cases. In this way, the introduction of the fixed fee system focused upon increasing time efficiency as a central feature of wider strategies to promote market-type mechanisms and approaches more generally.

The introduction of the fixed fee has had major ramifications, as subsequent sections of this chapter illustrate. There have been significant impacts on both the quantity and the quality of working time in Law Centres, with increasing pressures towards work intensification more generally.

Time pressures and work intensification

Law Centre workers and volunteers raised widespread concerns about the tensions and the associated dilemmas that the introduction of the fixed fee scheme involved in terms of time pressures. These pressures were particularly problematic for those involved with Law Centres that were entirely or almost entirely dependent upon the fixed fee scheme for their funding. (Law Centres with access to alternative funding sources, such as local authority funding, tended to have rather more flexibility, with correspondingly greater scope for staff to exercise discretion in relation to issues of time management.

The fixed fee system itself was associated with pressures either to do unpaid overtime in order to meet the requisite targets or to finish cases before they were fully resolved. As a caseworker noted, for example, "there wasn't enough time to do everything that needed to be done", adding that these time pressures left no "time available for other aspects of the work, such as working with the community".

A solicitor from a different Law Centre similarly argued that the pressures to make the fixed fee system work meant that people had to work a lot harder, come in earlier in the morning, stay longer in the afternoon and therefore work longer hours altogether – without getting paid for the additional hours. A worker from another Law Centre commented on his situation in similar vein, describing the transformation of his conditions of work caused by the increasing time pressures. Of recent years, he explained, he had had to "put in late nights to get things done". "You can see cracks", he reflected, emphasising the emotional and physical strains of the changes caused by the introduction of the fixed fee scheme. These were recurring themes, others describing similarly the effects of excessive working hours, along with the strains involved in meeting the targets.

Despite their efforts to comply with the new requirements while maintaining their ethos and values, there was widespread concern, among both Law Centre workers and other stakeholders, as to whether the quality of the service was suffering as a result. One Law Centre worker commented, for example, that this was particularly problematic for cases that involved "working in the community or when you are dealing with issues around violence, homelessness or immigration (…) where you have to go beyond that half an hour slot". In these cases it was necessary that "you give time to people in distressed situations and that was always one of the strengths within the voluntary sector. I hope that we do not lose this", she concluded, or the quality of service would be correspondingly reduced.

A young caseworker from another Law Centre commented in similar vein, reflecting that the time pressures made it impossible to "spend enough time preparing representation", so that "the amount of time we are spending with the clients is really limited". Despite her commitment to the ethos of providing comprehensive legal advice, these pressures and the increasingly precarious conditions of work made it impossible for her to develop personal plans for the future within the Law Centre, she concluded.

A related criticism was that financial pressures were incentivising Law Centres to cherry pick the cases that needed less time and could therefore yield surpluses more readily and rapidly. Although the LSC was firmly opposed to cherry picking, as has already been suggested, there were widespread fears that this would emerge as a significant problem. A Law Centre worker commented as follows on precisely this dilemma: "we don't cherry pick cases", adding that "we have problems turning people away". But, he reflected, this "could be our downfall", undermining the Law Centre's prospects for remaining financially viable under the fixed fee system.

Meanwhile the time pressures associated with the fixed fee system were being intensified even further by the increased amounts of time that Law Centre workers and volunteers reported as being needed in order to fulfil the new system's administrative requirements. The following section explores these administrative aspects in more detail.

Time efficiency: output versus outcome

Efforts to use time more efficiently, as the fixed fee scheme intended, were being offset by the time required to comply with the new accountability system, a number of Law Centre workers reflected. As a result, it was argued, there was less time to focus on the actual legal work. The time pressures were being compounded, in addition, by the fact that there were frequent changes to the procedures in question.

A solicitor who had left a Law Centre after working there for 27 years commented on these shifting administrative requirements in the following terms. When she had arrived at the Law Centre, she explained, "we were pretty efficient when only 20% of the Law Centre resources went into admin". By the time that she left the Law Centre she had needed to spend between 50% and 60% of her time in order to cope with the additional administrative burdens and what she described as the "very, very complex financial arrangements". This had been "utterly demoralising", in her view, precipitating her decision to leave the Law Centre.

Comparable experiences were shared by a number of others, who were similarly critical of the administrative requirements involved. As a result of these requirements, one solicitor commented, "a significant part of people's working time is now spent on doing tremendous amounts of paper work". These pressures were further intensified by the risk of not getting paid at all, if the LSC forms were not filled in correctly. A staff member from another Law Centre exemplified this by telling the story of a case in which she had omitted the date, when filling in the Legal Aid certificate. As a result, some two months' worth of legal work went unpaid.

In summary, while it was intended to increase efficiency and reduce the time spent per case, the fixed fee scheme was widely considered, on the contrary, to have increased the time that Law Centres needed to spend in order to fulfil the additional administrative requirements, leaving less time for doing the legal work itself.

Apart from the increasing amount of time required to administer Law Centres, there were many criticisms of the LSC's approach to defining time efficiency in the first place, in the context of the work that Law Centres were actually doing. Time efficiency should not simply be equated with a quantitative understanding of time. A reduction in the amount of time spent per case may reduce costs in the short term, it was suggested, but may prove to be an inefficient use of time in the longer term. Tensions between the outputs necessary to receive enough funding through legal aid contracts and more holistic and sustainable (long-term) outcomes were a recurring theme.

Time spent approaching clients' problems holistically was considered as time well spent, building relationships of trust with individuals and with organisations and groups within communities. This argument was reinforced by evidence from a study of advice service, by the Council on Social Action. Its published findings, *Time well-spent* (Council on Social Action, 2009), pointed to the transformative nature of personal advice relationships, arguing that time spent on building good relationships and listening to clients' problems was also making sense from a time-efficiency point of view. The authors concluded that 'it [spending time with clients] is not a luxury. Rather, it is instrumental to achieving a quality outcome and value for money' (Council on Social Action, 2009, p 29).

This was especially relevant when working with clients for whom English was not their first language. As one volunteer reflected, there were particular tensions here in attempting to balance the ethos and values of the Law Centre with the temporal restrictions that the requirements of the fixed fee imposed: "We couldn't do time limited appointments here. Because of the nature of the community we have here, English is not the first language of most people", which meant that "if you had twenty minutes with a client you wouldn't get past hello". Ultimately, such an approach would be a waste of time. As he concluded, "you would not be able to give them an effective service; the to and fro between interpreter and client takes time" – time well spent.

Others commented that "there were pressures to churn people through to manage the time pressures related to the fixed fee funding system, with less time to focus on the wider issues", such as doing preventative or policy work. There were increasing tendencies to adopt what some described as a "factory approach, more like a production line" – "more of a conveyor belt approach", a lawyer reflected, contrasting this with the more holistic approach to each individual client's needs that she considered to be more appropriate to the way in which Law Centres should operate.

There are parallels here with Sanderson and Sommerlad's anxiety that the implementation of differing work practices (as a result of the fixed fee system) may contribute to the rise of legal aid factories. This would enable a high number of cases to be closed quickly, in order to make the fixed fee work, they predicted, but would pose 'difficulties for many smaller agencies and firms, especially those committed to specialist and/or high-quality work' (Sanderson and Sommerlad, 2011, pp 192–3). Sanderson and Sommerlad suggested that this way of making the fixed fee system work would be possible only via the creation of a two-tier system with qualified legal executives, and unqualified clerks or paralegals employed at significantly lower rates of pay, thereby exacerbating the processes of deskilling and de-professionalisation.

In summary, the reforms that were being implemented, following the Carter report, were perceived as leading to the promotion of administrative systems that were reminiscent of Taylorist principles and practices of management, focused on measurable outputs, while minimising autonomy over work processes and time allocation for front-line staff. Before we come back to the discussion of how far these changes might be understood as the re-emergence of a Taylorist regime, the following section summarises debates about alternative approaches to notions of value and the measurement of value, time valued and the value of time in relation to the work of Law Centres.

Time valued and the value of time

Appreciations of the social and economic value of Law Centres were frequently expressed by stakeholders from organisations and agencies working with Law Centres, such as local authorities, CABs and other advice agencies. There were concerns, however, as to how a preventative approach could be integrated into the current funding system of the fixed fee. A number suggested that this all raised wider issues of measurement and value. As a project worker from an advice network pointed out, for instance, Law Centres were in fact undertaking work that was saving time on a systemic basis. This should be valued as time well spent.

Another stakeholder reflected similarly, pointing to the potentially negative effects if those who needed legal advice were to be unable to have access to it via Law Centres. There was a risk that the courts could become clogged up if people were not adequately represented and if unrepresented litigants failed to complete the requisite paper work effectively, he concluded. Time, including the court's time, would be wasted in cases where "papers would be sent back again and again".

As has already been suggested, the case for reviewing approaches to the relationship between efficiency and time was particularly evident in relation to the value of preventative work. Preventative work could help to identify interrelated problems and thereby make it possible to intervene, more effectively, at an early stage. But this was becoming increasingly untenable. As a solicitor explained, over recent years Law Centres had become "understandably focused upon fire-fighting rather than upon why fires were starting in the first place".

Similar statements concerning the value of preventative work were made by Law Centres' stakeholders. For example, a spokesperson from an organisation that provided funding for Law Centres commented on the pressures that were squeezing out preventative work, despite its value, and reflected on the problems of measuring this type of value. As she explained, people who seek advice from Law Centres "might come in with a housing issue but you find out that there's a health issue, there's an education issue, a whole raft of issues that the family is facing". "A little bit of help at the beginning", she continued, "could save the local authority an awful lot of time and effort and money towards the end." This type of approach, she recognised, was "something that is not very easy to measure though" (at least not in ways that would necessarily convince funders).

Law Centres had already addressed this question of measurement, back in the Thatcher era. The Law Centres Federation Evaluation Framework Research Team had set out to explore ways of *measuring what was of value* in their work, contrasting this with evaluation approaches that ended up *valuing what was being measured*. It produced a report in 1988 outlining its findings (Law Centres Evaluation Framework Team, 1988).

These questions of value and measurement subsequently became a topic of broader interest, as evidenced in a number of more recent publications, in the context of public service modernisation. 'Targets', as Milbourne and Cushman among others have pointed out, 'do more than require a level of performance: they structure discourse and define categories of what is meaningful and what is marginal' (Milbourne and Cushman, 2013, p 490). What actually constituted value in the advice sector was the question explored by the New Economics Foundation (NEF), for example (NEF Consulting, 2008; 2009; 2010a), together with the question of how outcomes in advice could be measured (NEF Consulting, 2010b), taking into account the outreach and preventative work that Law Centres had been committed to undertaking. The authors of one of the New Economic Foundation's studies (NEF Consulting, 2010a) questioned the assumptions of efficiency being made by the then current legal aid reforms. Their report argued that 'the concept of efficiency and competition in service delivery (...) isn't necessarily compatible with **best value** over the longer term' (NEF Consulting, 2010a, p 6). In contrast to the commodified understanding of legal advice – that is, an understanding that views legal advice as a commodity to be consumed – the authors proposed that the holistic services that Law Centres had been committed to providing were 'more consistent with a citizenship or social-change model of value' (NEF Consulting, 2010a, p 6).

These differing and often conflicting notions of time and of what constitutes value relate back to the wider debates that were raised at the beginning of this chapter.

Conclusion

This chapter has focused upon the ways in which the accountability and administrative systems that were introduced following the Carter report placed temporal pressures on Law Centres. Critics argued that the business model, which focused on the production of measurable outputs, failed to take into account the time that Law Centre workers and volunteers needed to spend on essential but not easily measurable or countable outputs. The resulting tensions became particularly evident in terms of the time needed for building and maintaining relationships with Law Centres' clients and in terms of the time needed for doing preventative and outreach work with surrounding communities. This raises questions about the extent to which such a neo-Taylorist model may be appropriate at all, as an approach to increasing efficiency in the provision of advice services, for the longer term.

These strategies led to intensifications of working time, the growth of excessive working hours and increasing time pressures in Law Centres, potentially demoralising staff in the process. Crowley et al (2010) have argued that there are parallels here with the wider impacts of the 'heightened performance pressures' of neo-Taylorist managerial practices and the ways in which they have 'impinged on the nature of professional work' (Crowley et al, 2010, p 441) – with potentially detrimental effects on the personal health and well-being of the staff concerned.

There were particular ironies here. It was not simply that neo-Taylorist approaches were potentially counter-productive in terms of promoting increasing operational efficiency sustainably. Neo-Taylorist approaches were also potentially counter-productive in terms of the possible impacts on staff motivation and morale. Alternative approaches to the management of human resources, such as the promotion of quality circles, had arguably been more effective as strategies for increasing productivity, in the private sector. There, the focus had been upon engaging employees positively, motivating them and promoting effective team working. The aim had been to improve quality as well as to increase productivity, thereby enhancing firms' competitiveness in an increasingly challenging economic climate. Such strategies had been widely considered in management debates in the 1980s, building upon what were believed to be key ingredients of the success of Japanese approaches to management (Bocker and Overgaard, 1982; Ross and Ross, 1982).

If governments were committed to importing private sector approaches into management, then these types of approaches might have been thought to have relevance as part of strategies to increase productivity and, most importantly, to improve the quality of public services. The pitfalls and perils of neo-Taylorist approaches have been well documented (Boyle, 2011). The irony was that it was neo-Taylorist strategies, rather than more forward-looking private sector strategies, that were imported into the management of public services via the public service modernisation agendas.

None of this is to suggest that time management is not an issue to be addressed; on the contrary, as one of the present authors reflected after visiting a busy CAB office where staff were working against the clock, trying to meet the needs of everyone waiting in the queue that snaked around the building. How to give each person sufficient time and still ensure that everyone received advice before the office had to close? The question is not whether but how such dilemmas are to be addressed.

The following chapter takes up the impact of public service modernisation agendas in terms of staff motivation and morale in Law Centres, focusing on their experiences and their reactions, either quitting or developing coping strategies in response. This then brings the discussion back, in the final chapter, to questions of value and values in the welfare state more generally, together with questions about alternatives to marketisation as strategies for providing public services more effectively – and with greater democratic accountability to service users, would-be service users and their wider communities.

Note
[1] For a general discussion on the emergence of time discipline and the importance of clock-time in the period of industrialisation see Thompson (1967).

EIGHT

Alienation and demoralisation, or continuing labours of love?

This chapter draws together evidence on the impact of the challenges and dilemmas of public service modernisation for the staff members and volunteers involved with Law Centres. As has already been suggested, one of the criticisms that has been levelled at New Public Management systems is that they presuppose negative views of human motivation, assuming that employees in general, and professionals more specifically, need the discipline of targets imposed from above (Le Grand, 2003). As a result, critics have argued, target-type cultures actually risk alienating public service workers, undermining the very motivations and commitments that brought them into the public service professions in the first place.

There is, in addition, evidence from research to suggest that such motivations and commitments to the public service ethos may be deeply rooted in professionals' own personal histories and identities (Hoggett et al, 2009). This can add to the dilemmas that are faced in the context of public service modernisation, dilemmas which may be experienced emotionally as well as in more practical ways. The term 'emotional labour' covers a range of meanings and usages, from varying perspectives. It could refer to employers' demands that service workers such as air stewardesses should keep smiling 'as though they really meant it' to reassure their passengers, constituting additional exploitation of the employees in question, it could be argued (Hochschild, 1983; Standing, 2011). But the term has also been applied to the emotional engagement of nurses, for example, giving of themselves emotionally as they care for seriously ill patients (Smith, 1999). It is in this latter sense that the term has been used to understand the particular dilemmas faced by public service workers in the contemporary policy context (Hoggett et al, 2009).

The first part of this chapter builds upon earlier discussions in relation to Law Centres' ethos and values, as outlined in Chapter Three, providing fuller accounts of people's motivations. This leads into the discussion of the ways in which people's motivations had been affected by the introduction of more marketised approaches to the provision of legal aid. As the discussion argues, there was evidence of considerable stress, including emotional stress and burn-out, together with some evidence of alienation and demoralisation. But this was only part of the picture, as the penultimate section of this chapter demonstrates on the basis of evidence from staff and volunteers alike. This leads into the final section, which summarises the coping strategies that were being adopted and the ways in which the public service ethos was, or was not, being maintained and reproduced.

Motivations and values

As previous chapters have already suggested, altruism may be combined with more self-interested motives, entwined with moral, social, psychological, religious and cultural influences. As Titmuss had argued in relation to the giving of blood, 'No donor type can, of course, be said to be characterized by complete, disinterested, spontaneous altruism' (Titmuss, 1970, p 89). Motivations among donors varied, although particular patterns did emerge. There were relatively straightforward expressions of the desire to help others, such as 'I felt it was a small contribution that I could make to the welfare of humanity' (Titmuss, 1970, p 227), for instance. Others referred to traditions of donating in their families, or to more general awareness of the need for the service. There were, in addition, expressions of gratitude and the desire to give something back, donating blood after 'being told that my own life had been saved by transfusion. Determined to repay' (Titmuss, 1970, p 228), the explanation of one woman, referring to her own experience in childbirth. Such notions of reciprocity and solidaristic interdependence have been central to debates on the welfare state, as has already been suggested.

Studies subsequent to Titmuss's have explored motivations and values among public service workers more specifically, as Chapter Three has already outlined in the context of debates on the public service ethos. Was working in the public services more than just a job? Here too the desire to benefit the community emerged as the most frequently cited goal in a survey of managers, for example (Steele, 1999), providing 'a common theme and sense of purpose for people working in local government, health and the police' (Steele, 1999, p 13).

Other parallels emerge, including the influence of childhood experiences and family patterns. Psycho-social approaches have explored such influences further, identifying the affective basis for commitments to social justice as well as to social care. A complex mixture of compassion and anger, Hoggett et al (2009) argue, 'fuels a reparative desire to undo the damage and suffering experienced by particular groups or communities, or, in Titmuss's terms, a desire to repair the texture of social relations' (Hoggett et al, 2009, p 81).

The point is absolutely not to suggest that public service workers are uniquely altruistic. Rather, the point, as previous chapters have already suggested, is to emphasise the importance of recognising the complexity and depth of their motivations and values. As Hoggett et al write, 'In our conversations with development workers we realised that a variety of different values and motivations underlay their commitment to what they did. We also began to realise how deeply held these were, how frequently earlier life experiences had nurtured a sensitivity to injustice and the compassion and anger that accompanied this' (Hoggett et al, 2009, p 83).

So how does this all apply to Law Centres? As Chapter Three has already outlined, there was – unsurprisingly – considerable overlap between the ethos and values of Law Centres and the motivations and values of those who worked in them, whether as paid staff or as volunteers. People chose to work in Law

Centres because this chimed with their own values and commitments to facilitating access to justice for all, "championing all who experience injustice at any level and by doing so giving people a chance to have their voice heard in society". A number of Law Centre staff mentioned their own personal backgrounds when explaining the strength of their motivation to engage with issues of social justice. One management committee member/trustee commented, for instance, that her father had been a vicar, and so she had grown up with the norm of supporting all those who had come to their door seeking help and advice, including those with problems such as homelessness. Similar references to the influences of parents were made by others whose home backgrounds were less directly touched by the types of problems that Law Centres address. For example, a lawyer who described his own background as having been privileged (having attended a public school) referred to the importance of the influence of his mother, who had always manifested empathetic concern for others (eventually becoming a social worker). More directly, another lawyer explained that "my dad had been an advice worker in his career", which had awakened her interest in a legal career in the not-for-profit sector.

As Chapter Three has also explained, some described their motivation in terms of their own commitments to social movements for social justice and anti-racism. A lawyer with experience of Law Centres reflected that "my motivation for working in Law Centres ... is bound up with my own biography", outlining his experiences of squatting and of defending those involved in squatting. As a result of working alongside the local Law Centre, he decided to pursue a legal career, seeing "the value of becoming a lawyer to provide legal services of this type". In more formal political terms, a lawyer working in another Law Centre explained that she had always had an interest in becoming a lawyer, but not in commercial practice, given her interest in progressive politics, including membership of the Labour Party, from her teens.

Others described the influence of more direct experiences of inequalities and disadvantages. A management committee member/trustee (with a different Law Centre from the one cited above) reflected on his "whole life dealing with social justice" as an active trade unionist whose own father had been blacklisted for trade union activities (taking up health and safety issues in the hot metal industry). For him, the issues that the Law Centre was taking up were "about a moral stance", about "right and wrong". Several other respondents similarly mentioned their family backgrounds – including the experience of having been with a parent on a picket line – and experiences that had been central to their developing commitment to social justice. "Working for the common good", as one case worker expressed it, after explaining that as a child he had taken sandwiches to his father on the picket line during the 1972 miners' strike. Working for the Law Centre made him happy, he added. "This is what I think I had been looking for ... [through his own trade union work and through previous public service jobs]: to try to help people."

It was clear that for a number of Law Centre workers their involvement with the Law Centre was central to their own identity and sense of self. A lawyer the majority of whose career had been in Law Centres reflected that "it [working in Law Centres] has become part of my self-image". He added that "if I went into private practice now I would be quite ashamed", given the contrast that he had himself experienced when working in the private sector for a short time after qualifying.

This personal identification was similarly demonstrated by a Law Centre worker who had been actively involved in setting up and working with a particular centre over a number of years. "This is my baby ... I love it ... it's part of my life", he commented, adding that others felt similar levels of commitment (including working without pay, at one point, when funding had been temporarily withdrawn). A lawyer in another Law Centre[1] provided yet another example, illustrating the ways in which the Law Centre was bound up with her own identity and sense of self. Explaining that "without a doubt" she planned to continue with this type of work in the Law Centre, she added that "I can't think of another place where I could find work where I can be who I want to be".

Motivation and gender

Given earlier feminist research on gender, work and caring (Finch and Groves, 1983; Ungerson, 1990), the research included an analysis in terms of gender. Were women more focused upon caring and/or less focused upon more traditionally male career trajectories, for example? More generally, the law has evidently been an increasingly popular career choice for women, with women making up some 64% of students enrolling on relevant law degrees (compared with 45% of the total of solicitors on the roll in 2008). Solicitors from ethnic minority backgrounds made up just over 10% of the roll, although here too the situation seemed to be changing, with just over 30% from ethnic minority backgrounds enrolling as law students. Progress was evidently being made, as Kennedy had already recognised, while pointing to the distance still to be travelled (Kennedy, 2005a). In terms of career trajectories to the most senior levels of the legal profession, there would still seem to be issues to be addressed in terms of equalities, for example, with women accounting for under 8% of **QCs** in the same period.

As it turned out, gender did not emerge as a significant factor in relation to the motivation to work in Law Centres. Appendix 1 includes information on such slight differences as did seem to emerge from the research.

As previous chapters have already illustrated, there were a range of comments on each topic both from men and from women. Comments on the value of time spent with clients were very similar as were comments on the pressures of trying to address complex issues with a client in no more than 30 minutes. It was a woman who argued that "you feel the need to be more business-like [in terms of the time spent with each client] but you can't do it like that – not when you're working with the community, not when you are dealing with issues maybe around violence or homelessness or immigration". But it was also a woman who commented on the importance of "an efficiencies approach" and added that 30 minutes should be plenty of time to undertake a professional analysis even when addressing complex problems.

As the rest of this chapter demonstrates, there were plenty of comments that testified to men's personal commitment and emotional involvement in their work, just as there were plenty of comments demonstrating such commitments among women.

Of course this does not in any way prove that gender differences were not at work, and simply clarifies that this particular research did not provide sufficient evidence to identify any such patterns. This may perhaps give some clues as to the characteristics of many of the men who were choosing to work or volunteer in Law Centres. But this would be to speculate beyond the scope of the evidence in question.

Nor did this research investigate the extent to which Law Centres' services had been particularly important to women as clients – with correspondingly greater impacts on women if the scope of legal aid were further reduced. The likely gender impact of the proposed legislative changes has been central to these debates more widely. As Stephenson and Harrison's (2011) study pointed out, 62% of applications for civil legal aid were being made by women, with higher percentages in areas such as education and family law. Cuts in legal aid would have significant impacts on women, including in relation to welfare benefits, housing, immigration and aspects of domestic violence (Stephenson and Harrison, 2011). But this aspect – of the wider impacts on women – was also beyond the remit of this particular project.

Comparing and contrasting Law Centres with working in other sectors and types of agency

As Chapter Three has suggested, a number of those involved, both men and women, picked up on the theme of the particular ethos and values of Law Centres as a motivation for their involvement. For some, there were comparisons to be drawn between working in Law Centres and their previous experiences in other agencies. Several commented on the similarities, describing their work in the Law Centre as building upon previous experiences in related areas of work, such as working with refugees, migrant workers and asylum seekers, managing a refuge for those affected by domestic violence or working on homelessness. In addition, the manager of one Law Centre said that she had also managed advice provision in the region and so had relevant background, knowing how important these issues were and how they related to wider issues, including equalities issues. The manager of another Law Centre made a comparable reference to the relevance of her experience in previous posts, adding that this was the most challenging of a series of challenging posts. There were parallels with the comments of a number of those involved as trustees/management committee members, several of whom had previous experience as trustees of other public service organisations. In each of these instances, the underlying motivations and values echoed the public service values expressed above, emphasising the similarities, despite some differences in context.

For others, however, there were sharp contrasts to be drawn with their previous experiences elsewhere, experiences that had drawn them into becoming involved with Law Centres instead. A lawyer who had previously worked as a clerk in a private firm of solicitors commented that "it was all about making money". "I came here [to the Law Centre] because I love the work", he added. "When I've done a case [successfully] I've changed someone's life." Another lawyer, who had experience of working in Washington, DC in the 1970s, explained that in his view "if you were a millionaire you got your case done properly, and if you were a ten millionaire your problem was solved by a telephone call to the White House", "so I came back and decided that this [practising in the private sector] wasn't the career for me".

A young student undertaking a placement with a Law Centre offered a comparable although more contemporary view. "All that we heard at Uni was commercial, commercial, commercial", she reflected. Since she was placed with the Law Centre, her "eyes opened". She would be taking this wider understanding of "what goes on in the real world" and her wider understanding of the law and how it impacts on people's lives with her, into her future career. This comment links to the findings on the dynamic ways in which motivations and values can develop over time, as Chapter Three has already suggested.

Before we move on to this, however, it should be added that dissatisfaction with the private sector was not the only factor in such choices. A Law Centre worker commented that he had come from advice work in a voluntary sector organisation in the same locality. This was a large organisation which he described as working in ways that he found personally unsympathetic, in terms of his own motivation and values. "It was very corporate", in his view, he explained (reflecting, perhaps, increasing marketisation within the voluntary sector more generally and contrasting this unfavourably with the more congenial ethos of the Law Centre to which he had moved).

Motivation and values: a two-way process

As Chapter Three has already suggested, motivations and values can be strengthened – or, indeed, undermined – by people's experiences. There were examples of people's having become involved in Law Centres by happenstance – applying for a job or a traineeship, or applying to become a volunteer because the opportunity presented itself. Sometimes this opportunity appealed because the person concerned was already sympathetic to the work of Law Centres, as with the trustee/management committee member who became involved as a trades council representative, responding to calls for a volunteer to take this on.

In other cases, though, those concerned had very little prior knowledge or understanding of the work of Law Centres. This was the case, for instance, with an administrative worker who had previously worked in the private sector. The person in question described herself as having become "passionate about the Law Centre now". She had become more involved as she saw "the impact on clients". "Without the Law Centre, clients just wouldn't have access to justice." If the Law Centre were to close, she concluded, she didn't know whether she could return to working in the private sector, and commented that she "wouldn't have said that before [working in the Law Centre]". There were a number of similar examples.

These included lawyers providing pro bono advice sessions. Many of them came with existing commitments to "widening access to justice" and "contributing to the community". Another long-standing volunteer explained that volunteering was rooted in her values: "I've always had a social conscience and a belief in justice". But there were also examples of others who came, initially, with other motivations, in some cases largely because this was being encouraged by their line managers. One lawyer explained that voluntary work in Law Centres was seen as being very useful because they provided wide experience, in contrast with the more limited experience available in private firms that might be more reluctant to allow a young lawyer, let alone a trainee, to undertake responsible work for their corporate clients.

A lawyer who had begun to volunteer early in his career provided an example of how he had been encouraged by his firm to undertake some voluntary work. This, he suggested, may have been for a variety of reasons, from commitment to corporate social responsibility to the promotion of his chambers' public image, and also as what he described as a "promotional device" for his employers. Once he had started volunteering, however, he came to the view that "this was something that fits naturally for me". It had become "very important for me to do the Law Centre work", which he enjoyed. He had been doing it for a number of years now and planned to continue with it until he retired. This was basically because "it's a good thing to do. People should help each other", he explained. This was central to his view of society, which was based upon people helping each other in mutually supportive ways rather than being simply focused upon profit making. As Chapter Three has already suggested, individuals can and indeed do demonstrate public service motivation, whether they work in the public, voluntary or private sectors – despite differences between the sectors in terms of their organisational aims more generally.

Pathways through from client to volunteer and from volunteer to paid professional

There were also examples of former clients who had been motivated to become volunteers and, in some cases, qualified professionals as a result of their initial involvement with a Law Centre. One lawyer explained, for example, that she had first come to the Law Centre to seek advice as a law student and single parent with a problem in relation to housing benefit. This had been some 12 years previously. She had begun to volunteer for a couple of days a week while completing her degree, and then worked at the Law Centre as a locum. She had obtained a training contract (at another Law Centre) and was now employed as a senior solicitor, back in the same office where she had first become involved. So the Law Centre had been central to the pathway that she had taken into the profession.

Similarly, a lawyer in another Law Centre explained that he had been working in manufacturing industry in the 1990s but had experienced problems with his rent sometime around 1995–96. As a result, he had gone to his local Law Centre for advice and had been helped. "This was when it [his involvement in Law Centres] started." He decided upon a career change and by 1997 he was studying law, completing his professional training and qualifying in 2005. He became a volunteer at the local Law Centre while studying, and subsequently obtained a job there. Apart from a period of training in a city law firm, he had worked in Law Centres ever since.

He described his motivation as "wanting to help others" as he himself had been helped. People in Law Centres were "passionate" in their commitment. As a client he had found that people in Law Centres "listened to me" and "believed in what I'm saying". This, together with the passion and commitment, was central to the distinctive ethos of Law Centres, in his view. As he later explained in more detail, this distinctive ethos had been challenged as a result of changes over the previous two years, leading him to decide to leave, and raising issues that are explored in more detail in the following section. But this is to leap ahead of the argument.

Meanwhile there were further examples of volunteers going on to qualify as lawyers as a result of their experiences. A lawyer in yet another Law Centre explained that he had started his legal career as a volunteer receptionist. This had been almost accidental, as he had not been thinking of a legal career, but through his involvement in the Law Centre his "passion grew". Qualifying as a legal executive encouraged him to go on and try to become a solicitor and, through the Law Centre, he obtained the opportunity to train. Such training opportunities provided pathways into the profession that were valued by people who would have otherwise struggled to qualify professionally, including a number of former Law Centre volunteers as well as a number of former clients.

Impacts of the Carter reforms

So far this chapter has focused upon the more positive aspects of people's motivations and values. But there was also evidence of more negative trends.

These included some very sad reflections such as the following: "I find that the uncertainty and instability of on-going funding and the high demands to meet funders' criteria (especially LSC) means that I am now less inclined to continue in a Law Centre". Another referred to feeling that "the role would be 'dumbed down' ... if I accepted the terms of the 'Carter Report' and remained employed I may become cynical and disillusioned with my role", adding that "despite a mortgage and being a sole earner, I remained true to my principles" (that is, deciding to resign) and concluding with some irony that "the role was subsequently deemed redundant" in any case. "I have begun to suffer from compassion fatigue", wrote another. "There is an increased level of hopelessness", added a third.

So, as well as comments about increasing motivation and engagement, there were also some disturbing accounts of demotivation, including accounts from people who were considering leaving their Law Centre. Some spoke of their extreme reluctance to leave the Law Centre, even though they either were contemplating this or had done so already. Typically, they explained that they felt constrained to do so as a result of funding uncertainties and/or, in some cases, of sensing a loss of vision, fearing that Law Centres were drifting away from their original mission in their struggles to meet the requirements of the current funding system. "You know you want to help people", one of those interviewed explained, "you want to help the community, you are there because you don't want to make profit like a private firm, you want to make a difference and it seems that the government is trying to squeeze that out of the community." This particular solicitor was moving on from the Law Centre to work for another not-for-profit organisation.

These accounts of demoralisation as a result of the Carter reforms are, of course, very personal. Deciding to leave a job in a Law Centre represented one end of the spectrum, and there were a number of examples of people who had done or who were in the process of doing precisely that. Another lawyer (who had also been a trainee) made similar comments about the impact of the reforms. "I think in terms of [my experiences as] an employee [these changes] really demotivated me." As a result of the changes, "rather than providing a personal service and trying to help someone who may be very vulnerable [with] no other access for them to legal services ... instead you are doing a paper exercise, you are not giving a personal service, it's impersonal, it's rush, there is less satisfaction in the work we do".

This lawyer went on to explain that she had reluctantly decided to leave (and subsequently left), believing that the new LSC contract would involve further pressures. She added that "I think what all staff found was that the quality is suffering". Other staff would leave too, in her opinion. "They really believe in the principles of the Law Centre and that's what attracted them. It's just the working environment has changed. We've got a really good team of people. I think you have to be quite selfless perhaps wanting to be working for a Law Centre. You are considering other people, you are not necessarily wanting to work for that flashy law firm ... our office is historically in a very deprived area. So it takes a certain kind of person to want to work there in any type of capacity, or be in the management committee. I think you want to do some good and those kind of people are just gonna walk away because they are thinking 'what's the point'?" She had taken up a post in another not-for-profit agency.

One of the major fears, then, was that the pressures would actually lead to a worse service for clients. Reflecting on the problems of working on what she described as "a shoe string" (having to rely on legal texts handed down from sympathetic colleagues in private firms, for instance), one lawyer explained that she sometimes felt as if she was operating on a "wing and a prayer". So far, the quality of service had been maintained, despite this, but if this were to change and if "it starts to actually show (e.g. with a claim for negligence) I'll throw in the towel". This was a fear, although the Law Centre was still coping, for the present, in her view.

A lawyer in a different Law Centre had actually reached the point of contemplating a change of career, worrying as to whether she would find that she couldn't do what she described as "a decent job for my client". That, she concluded was "something I wouldn't have dreamed of five years ago". A similar comment was made by another lawyer who had decided to move on to another post (in a related field). Having referred to the pressures on the job and the difficulties of meeting client needs, she concluded that this all "took you so far away from what you wanted to do and what people actually need". "So I suppose if you asked five years ago, I couldn't have seen a time where I was anything else than a Law Centre lawyer or possibly a civil legal aid lawyer doing social justice, but I can't make it work anymore, so I quit."

There were parallels with some of the comments made by trustees/management committee members. One long-standing member of a management committee reflected that she was unsure of her own future involvement. Although she had maintained her involvement over a number of years (including some periods that had been described as challenging, to say the least) she felt that "much more is expected of management committees". She added that "I feel it's almost semi-professional", requiring a different skill set, rather than the local knowledge and skills that she had brought as a community activist and trade unionist.

At the other end of the spectrum from those who had left, there were those who were absolutely committed to staying, whatever the personal cost, either financially or emotionally. Despite the pressure, one lawyer explained that she coped because "you just pop on a few more hours", adding that "I don't mind doing that". "Everyone feels the same." These could be described as "labours of love", unpaid work for the love of it. "I've always been passionate about my work." This was, in her view, in contrast to those in large organisations where, "come 5 o'clock they're out the door", whether or not a particular piece of work needed to be completed. In the Law Centre, on the other hand, "it's very nice to be around people with the same passion for work, the same passion for people".

One of her colleagues made similar comments, adding that if funding were to be lost in future she would "do something else for an income" and then continue to "run an advice session anyway ... I'll do that on a voluntary basis as a labour of love". A lawyer with many years' experience in another Law Centre similarly commented that, with a family and a mortgage, he would need to find paid employment if the Law Centre were to run out of funding, but he would be personally committed to continuing to provide advice on a pro bono basis.

The public service ethos was clearly alive, then, although at considerable cost to the individuals concerned. The job was demanding enough in any case. As one young volunteer commented, it was not just about spending time with clients but also about "lots of blood, sweat and tears". There was evidence of burn-out, together with evidence of levels of stress that could well lead to burn-out. And there were also some very practical reflections on the limits of what could be achieved by voluntary efforts alone. Although one particular Law Centre had continued to operate on a voluntary basis for a period, until funding had been restored, this would be unsustainable in the current context, it was pointed out. Apart from any other factors, workers would be unlikely to be able to live on benefits while providing the service on a voluntary basis, as they had managed to do previously. In the past, people had expressed willingness to make considerable sacrifices in order to keep the service going. But rents and mortgages still needed to be paid.

Coping with tensions and stress

As earlier chapters and the previous section have suggested, both staff and management committee members provided illustrations of how stressful the changes actually were, in their experience. Among the sharper examples was the case of a Law Centre where staff had collectively decided to take a pay cut (despite being aware of the problems this might cause for some staff, particularly those with family commitments). Making staff redundant had clearly been stressful for management committees too, as well as for the staff involved, as were decisions about changing staff conditions of service such as maternity leave, in order to make savings. Being in what felt like a "state of crisis" was stressful, in any event. People spoke of feeling trapped by the challenges of survival from day to day, without the time to focus upon longer-term solutions. A number pointed to what they identified as "worrying levels of stress" as a result of these insecurities.

However, some referred to finding ways of managing their time more effectively. There were also references to the need to learn from time management practices in the private sector. One lawyer reflected that "you've got to have targets ... and a private mentality" in order to survive. He himself had worked in the private sector for a period precisely in order to acquire these skills, which he had then brought to the Law Centre when a job had come up there.

Others referred to the reality that Law Centre clients could also be challenging, "exasperating at times". Given that there were people with addiction issues and mental health issues among Law Centres' clients, and given that clients were likely to be stressed already when they came to seek legal advice, this was not surprising. Ways of coping with challenging behaviours included the use of humour – and sharing experiences with colleagues afterwards – to manage situations without impacting on the service to clients. "We just laugh it off" with colleagues afterwards, one manager explained when discussing ways of coping with challenging behaviours from clients.

So people were adopting a range of strategies in response to the stress. Good team work was frequently cited as a source of support. "We do try to support each other", an administrative worker explained, adding that if someone was really under pressure "then everyone rallies round and gives them the space they need". "A fantastic support network among staff", commented someone from another Law Centre. "It's stressful but this is a nice environment" a lawyer in yet another Law Centre commented, "sharing ideas, getting suggestions", with good levels of support between colleagues from other agencies as well as from the Law Centre itself. There were also references to regional groups of colleagues from other Law Centres and from the LCF, for instance.

Some also spoke more personally about their strategies for coping with stress. For example, a management committee member/trustee explained how she set out to distinguish those issues where it was possible to make some impact from those where it was not feasible, and then how "to stop anguishing about the latter" – easier said than done, in practice, it was agreed. Another respondent explained that he did "a lot of running" to relieve the stress, adding that he still felt depressed sometimes – and angry too, in the face of "commissioners who don't really understand the impact of what they are doing", whereas basically "all we want to do is to advise people".

Demoralisation and/or the social reproduction of continuing 'labours of love'?

So, was there evidence that the public service ethos was being undermined? In summary, as the previous section has demonstrated, there was clearly evidence of demoralisation and stress, leading some of those interviewed to decide to leave their jobs or to stop serving on management committees. Those who were taking such decisions seemed to be doing so with considerable reluctance, though. Demoralisation seemed to be generally linked to frustration at the difficulties in providing clients and communities with the types of services that they needed, rather than with any more fundamental rejection of the ethos and values of Law Centres per se. Realistically, funding insecurities were a factor in such decisions, as some of those who have been quoted above pointed out. There was widespread recognition that voluntary efforts would not be able to fill the gaps if funding were withdrawn. But none of this suggested any wholesale retreat from public service values more generally.

On the contrary, there was plenty of evidence to suggest that individuals and groups were providing unpaid labour, often to a considerable degree, in order to keep services going in challenging times. For some this was exacting a toll in terms of personal stress, with evidence of stress-related sickness and some evidence of potential burn-out. Much of the work was inherently stressful in any case, and there were other causes of stress to be considered too. But public service modernisation, as introduced with the Carter reforms, was adding new levels of stress, which were being compounded because of the emotional commitments and values of so many Law Centre workers and volunteers.

Previous research (Burdett, 2004) suggested that the motivations, values and commitment that long-established Law Centre workers demonstrated were likely to prove to be passing phenomena. Burdett raised concerns as to whether the next generation of 'Thatcher's children'[2] could be expected to be motivated in very different, more instrumental and far more individualistic ways. This was certainly the view expressed by a number of long-established public service professionals in other client-facing positions (Hoggett et al, 2009).

There was some evidence that long-established professionals harboured such fears for the future of the public service ethos. Several spoke of their concerns, as younger people were perceived as being far more individualistic and far more instrumental in their attitudes towards their jobs, lacking the types of commitment and political understanding that had been characteristic of earlier generations of Law Centre staff and volunteers. The next generation was "very different" in the view of one of those interviewed, for instance. They were "not as political, not as idealistic" and a "whole lot more sensible" (in terms of their attitudes towards their future careers).

A young lawyer in the same Law Centre echoed this last point insofar as she recognised a generational difference when it came to attitudes to funding and job security. She explained that younger people like herself tended to be more used to the fact that jobs were so often short term – precarious employment was the norm. (She was on short-term funding herself.) In her view, though, this did not mean that younger people were less committed than people who had joined Law Centres in the past. Older people typically had very strong principles. Their experiences were different from those of younger people. But younger people did also develop commitment, too. The young lawyer herself appreciated the ethos and values of the Law Centre, which she described as being "very principled here". There was "a real belief in some of the old fashioned principles ... about access to advice ... quality of the advice" for all, regardless of ability to pay.

Summarising generational differences, a manager from another Law Centre described some of its young legal volunteers as "really brilliant". There were some differences from those who came to work in Law Centres in the early days, the 1970s and 1980s, many of whom had been more politicised, perhaps. The younger staff and volunteers tended to come with what the manager described as rather less of a "political perspective" (implying perhaps that they tended not to start from a coherent political analysis of the underlying structural barriers to be overcome in order to be effective in promoting strategies for social justice). But the lack of an underpinning political perspective did not mean that younger staff and volunteers were interested only in casework, in her view. On the contrary, they were also interested in campaigning on justice issues. Their experiences of working in the Law Centre also broadened their appreciation of some of the problems that people actually faced. "'Now I get it', they'd say", the manager added. One of the present authors overheard a young volunteer in the same Law Centre make precisely such a comment, as he explained how and why he was involved in activities related to the Justice for All campaign.

Nor did there seem to be a problem, in terms of young people's interests, in pursuing legal careers with an emphasis upon access to justice. One of the universities that specialised in providing opportunities for learning through hands-on experience illustrated this with reference to the competition for places. They were vastly over-subscribed – which seemed to indicate that these representatives of the next generation were not at all uninterested or unmotivated. There would seem to be parallels here with John and Johnson's (2008) findings on the lack of clarity on generational differences, as discussed in Chapter Three.

In summary, some forms of the public service ethos seemed to be surviving and to be being transmitted to the next generation. But there was also evidence that this was being achieved at considerable cost in terms of stress and potential burn-out, labours of love and blood, sweat and tears.

Notes
[1] The Law Society, http://juniorlawyers.law society.org.uk, accessed 25 February 2012.

[2] The term 'Thatcher's children' has been used to imply that young people who were brought up in and just after the years when Margaret Thatcher was prime minister were socialised into a relatively individualistic, competitive and private market-orientated cultural climate.

NINE

Access to justice for disadvantaged communities: value and values

Access to justice was central to the principles upon which the post-war welfare state was established, as Chapter One explained, demonstrating the importance of Law Centres' contributions to the provision of access to justice for all, regardless of the ability to pay. How, then, were public service modernisation agendas being experienced in this vitally important but relatively under-researched field? And what might be the wider implications for social justice agendas more generally?

As the Introduction explained, Law Centres were selected for study for a number of reasons, including the fact that they were offering precisely the access to information about rights and responsibilities that had been identified as centrally important to the public service modernisation agendas, agendas through which governments have been aiming to shift the balance of power and accountability from public service providers towards more active and informed citizens and service users. Were these policy agendas facilitating the development of new forms of professionalism? Or, conversely, were they being experienced as promoting new forms of de-professionalisation (Banks, 2004), demotivating, demoralising and potentially undermining the occupational values and identities of those involved in Law Centres' work?

There are parallels here with wider debates. As Clarke and others have pointed out, public service modernisation has been posing major challenges as different aspects of the public realm have been subjected to processes of dissolution (Clarke, 2004). Although these processes have themselves been subjected to refusals and negotiations, as professionals and others have engaged in strategies of resistance, the extent to which they have been successful has been the subject of debate (Clarke, 2004; Kolthoff, Huberts and Heuvel, 2007), with continuing arguments about the ethical implications, and debates about the implications for professionalism in public services.

More specifically, in what ways were these changes being managed; what strategies were being adopted to cope with competing pressures and demands while maintaining professional ethical standards; how might strategies to respond to public service modernisation vary in differing settings; and what might be the implications for professional education and continuing professional development? There were issues here with potential relevance for debates on the future of the public service ethos and the future of the welfare state more generally.

Previous chapters have examined the evidence, illustrating the dilemmas and tensions that have been identified and some of the strategies that have been adopted, as Law Centre staff and volunteers have attempted to address the challenges while maintaining Law Centres' ethos and their own professional values. As previous chapters have also explained, Law Centres' ethos and values have been closely linked with the motivations and values of those who have been involved with them, whether as paid staff or as volunteers. This helps to explain why the dilemmas inherent in managing the challenges were being experienced so painfully, in so many cases. Before we summarise these findings and their possible implications for debates about the public service ethos and values more generally, this chapter reflects on the evidence for the value of Law Centres themselves. What claims were they making, and how far were these claims being corroborated by other stakeholders?

The value of Law Centres

> Law Centres are embedded in their communities and answer to committees of local people. They assist vulnerable people when they suffer injustice, educate people about their rights and tackle local problems. (Law Centres Federation website: www.lawcentres.org.uk)

This assertion was corroborated by stakeholders. A volunteer lawyer whose law firm encouraged its employees to undertake a range of pro bono work explained the need for Law Centres as follows:

> "I think there are certain things that society thinks people are entitled to: shelter, food are the obvious ones but at some point the right to be treated fairly comes along and the only way you can enforce that is through the law. You get some people who have been treated terribly and that is only prevented if people have recourse to the law. This is the system that ensures fairness, or what passes for fairness. I think if you can pay for the services you should but I guess it is often the people who can't pay who really need the law for fairness. I guess a society without legal representatives is a society without the law because the rules just mean nothing, don't they. If you don't know what you are entitled to and you don't follow the paths to get what you are entitled to, then it is as if the law did not exist."

As this law firm volunteer proceeded to point out, without Law Centres, democratic rights exist only on paper, rather than being genuinely available. This links back to the discussion in Chapter One of the central importance of access to justice as a defining characteristic of the post-war welfare state. One of the defining characteristics of Law Centres was the virtually universal appreciation for the work they did in providing access to justice. A former client testified to this:

> "Finding the Law Centre was like winning the Lottery. For me I think they're the people's lawyer, the poor people's lawyer. They represent the

people who cannot afford it and they fight for these people. Because in their view we've got rights just like the people who've got the money and we're entitled to the same thing as the people that have got the money".

Appreciation of Law Centres by other advice agencies across the statutory and voluntary sector was strongly evidenced from the stakeholder interviews. These agencies saw the Law Centres' *sine qua non* as being "accessible to all". An advice worker whose agency collaborated closely with their local Law Centre reflected: "The uniqueness of the Law Centre is that it is actually accessible to all. You can be anyone, which is really good. If you haven't got any money you can access the Law Centre and because it is a community based organisation you see all sorts of people there."

This was central to Law Centres' ethos. The advice worker explained that the Law Centre's ambience was welcoming and informal, which meant that "you feel you can relax and express yourself a little bit more", adding that "being in that environment it does make a difference".

> "If there isn't an organisation like the Law Centre available to people then where do people go? What do people do then? Is that not a form of concern for the government; that there are people who are abandoned and unsupported? Quite often people will just stay in their circumstances which isn't good because they are not getting the legal support, which is not ethical, it is not right, because of your situation, because you can't access a service. It brings in a hierarchy thing, with society, how all those who can actually afford it, their needs will be met, but those who can't ... their needs will not be met and it leaves a hole."

A local authority manager was also quick to emphasise the ways in which Law Centres could lead to improved managerial outcomes:

> "With homelessness, when it comes to challenging the outcome of our decision, we can't do that. Advice will have to be given by an independent person or group who would look at issues and satisfy themselves as to the necessity for such a challenge. Overall the Law Centre will stand guard on behalf of the individual and say, 'you know what, this is not compliant with the necessary requirements of the law, you have fallen short of what you set out to deliver, you need to rectify this, otherwise you face a challenge in court'. And for the most part the local authority [will] turn around and review their decision and see whether they were right. But usually at that point, justice is seen to be done because they reconsider more carefully".

The dual outcome of improved access to services and justice was thus being achieved.

However, for a young volunteer who was seeking work experience at a local Law Centre after graduating from college, what most stood out was the humanity and commitment encountered in a Law Centre:

> "You're likely to be helped here. You will be helped to the best of their ability and people will do the best they can and considering the budget and the pressures that they have to go by, they do a lot for the people that come in. They're very understanding, and the language barrier sometimes, the effort that is put in to find an interpreter, little things like that. It's all that extra effort that you won't get anywhere else, that easily. Especially considering that some of the people here are not being paid and there are a lot of volunteers. To put that effort in, knowing that you're not actually getting any money from it, that's a rare thing. You just feel like you're being cared for, you do. You feel like you're getting the help you need, because to go somewhere else, you're not going to get it and you're just going to be struggling. They are actually here for the community. That's what they're supposed to do and they do what they're meant to do."

The holistic approach of Law Centres was also particularly valued. For example, a local council manager spoke of the nature of the added value engendered by the local Law Centre in the following terms:

> "So usually the Law Centre would look at the whole issues concerning the person's circumstances and examine all of the parameters set down and satisfy themselves [as to whether] the local authority [has] done all they are required to do by law. Is there any more information from the individual that they have not bothered to interrogate or even ask the individual to provide? It is essential to continue to make reasonable inquiries, not just slap-dash inquiries."

The local council manager feared that without this independent oversight and intervention processes too often became cursory and inattentive. Rather than defensively interpreting the challenging questions asked of his department he argued such enquiries were "essential". By looking at the "whole issues" and asking the questions that the local authority had not "bothered to ... ask", the Law Centre broadened the reach of the law and the efficacy of the service and enhanced access to justice. From the client's point of view it was the way they were dealt with holistically, as well as with warmth, that made all the difference.

In addition to providing access to justice for individuals and communities who would otherwise have no recourse to the law, Law Centres were also valued for providing a wide range of specialist knowledge and skills. Chapter

Six has demonstrated the potential value of partnership working, when Law Centres were working collaboratively with other agencies. These benefits were identified by stakeholders who commented on the multiple benefits accrued from collaboration, notably in the provision of seamless services and capacity building across a local area.

Law Centres were valued for their contributions in a number of these ways, including leading on joint working initiatives, servicing interagency forums and providing bespoke training for advice workers. The synergies that arose from networking across organisational boundaries were highly prized by both statutory and voluntary sector colleagues. As one advice worker explained:

> "Organisations like [ours] are reliant on Law Centres to inform us about consultations which are out. It may even be preparing a template for a consultation response, so that the responses go in. The voluntary sector does not have time to do this because they are busy providing frontline services. It is important for the sector to be mobilised, represent our communities and have a voice."

This advice worker then cited the importance of the local Law Centre's value base and proven leadership:

> "They come from a very anti-racist, anti-sexist perspective. They have that ethos embedded in them in terms of what they do on a day-to-day basis. It's not an afterthought; it's not something that we could say they're not going to be looking at that point. They've got that political awareness. They understand the whole political context of why they were here in the first place and what they need to be doing. And they've held onto that and I suppose that's one of the reasons they're finding it difficult to hold on, like everybody else really. I always remember going to a Voluntary Sector Forum meeting and everyone's very formal and the [Law Centre] worker would speak up and challenge. They had the confidence to do that. For another organisation this may be difficult. The worker put their head above the parapet, put it that way in order to make their point and we have a lot of admiration and a lot of respect for that."

The implementation of the Carter reforms had been associated with significant reductions in the time spent on anything other than case work. But there was also some evidence that Law Centres were continuing to find ways of contributing to wider policy and preventative work. Where preventative and policy work was still taking place there was also evidence that it was being valued by other stakeholders. One council procurement officer illustrated this point, giving an example of the dilemmas involved in making a review of funding:

> "If we were to cut some of the services that our third sector [agencies such as the Law Centre] deliver we potentially will see an increase of people coming to see us for advice. That's one side, and without the prevention early on, for example on homelessness, we would be having to potentially pick those clients up and put them into some form of temporary accommodation. That has an impact on our stats and our ability to deliver and increases our costs. So you take from one end and you're actually increasing at the other end and there's a tightrope there in terms of balancing prevention with statutory functions. That all needs to be taken account of as part of the review."

The preventative work of Law Centres has had both social and economic value, as Chapter Seven argued in more detail. By feeding back intelligence into legal and partnership frameworks, for example, systems and performance measures could be improved, including avoiding unnecessary litigation. While these contributions were valued by stakeholders, there was also widespread recognition that these benefits might no longer be available in the future. As a local council manager recalled:

> "Over the years I've noticed that the Law Centres have blossomed into a group of community centres whereby legal advice can be obtained, social policy issues can sometimes be championed. But the near disappearance of legal aid to them has shackled their activities completely – it is almost killing off the services they provide in the various community groups. Some of them are shutting down and most people are threatened with their closures. So in an absence of adequate funding either through private individual contribution, or charitable groups, then Law Centres are set to disappear. It would be a sad case if that happens in this country because we have this tradition of very good Law Centres ... It would be really sad if they all disappeared because of lack of funding or changing government policy or local authority funding."

A funder explained that times of austerity made Law Centres especially vulnerable to closure, however:

> "In the past [Law Centres] have not been popular ... with some local authorities. Sometimes the officers are enlightened and see the opportunity to learn from feedback. It is often perhaps about convincing councillors who are going to have somebody knocking on the door saying 'don't close my library'. I often think that sometimes, if you are faced with cuts, like the authorities are now, the challenging situation may not be as welcomed; less staff, less time, less money ... I think that there is a fear from the Law Centres that that could be

more of an issue in the future and when they do challenge they are not popular and when they do this [in the context of austerity policies] they'll become even less popular. There is a view, I don't know how true it is, that the Citizens Advice Bureaux get more funding than Law Centres because Law Centres are more challenging towards the local authority. It is more in terms of professional legal advice, which CABs also do but sometimes it is more generalist."

But Law Centres were the linch-pins of strategic approaches to advice service provision. A local authority officer in one city explained that "they fit into the network and they are a city-wide service, although they do work sometimes with particular groups. The service is complementary, a specialist service that isn't met elsewhere. The other advice services give advice, the Law Centre gives specialist legal advice that isn't available elsewhere."

An advice worker from a neighbouring agency reflected in similar vein that "I really don't know what we'll do if they [the Law Centre] don't survive the next round of cuts".

"Save our Law Centres, they are crucial", another stakeholder concluded.

Ways forward facing uncertain futures?

Although there was evidence of considerable demoralisation among Law Centre staff and volunteers, there was also powerful evidence of continuing commitment. Despite their negative experiences, those who were most critical of public service modernisation agendas were among the ones who were also most determined to find ways forward, working smarter without losing sight of Law Centres' ethos and without compromising their own professional values. But there were stressful dilemmas to be faced, it emerged, and painful choices to be made in the context of the proposed – and subsequently enacted – legislation to restrict the provision of legal aid still further. This would have the effect of moving legal aid decisively away from 'a safety-net legal service working like a fifth pillar of the Welfare State', critics argued, and towards a minimalist 'rump service to cover people accused of a crime and civil cases for the poorest in which human rights were directly engaged' (Hynes, 2012, p 100). Considerable emotional labour was being expended as Law Centre staff and volunteers struggled to hold on to their values in face of these challenges, as previous chapters have already demonstrated.

Previous research had suggested that earlier generations of Law Centre staff and volunteers had been characterised by stronger commitments to Law Centres and to public service values overall. In contrast, younger generations were becoming more instrumental in their outlook, it had been suggested, and less troubled by the dilemmas of public service modernisation and marketisation agendas more generally (Burdett, 2004). These trends were not so clearly identified by this research, however. There were indeed some generational differences, as earlier chapters have demonstrated. But there were also examples of younger staff and volunteers demonstrating strong commitments; commitments that were typically strengthened further as a result of these people's experiences in Law Centres.

Education and training for future generations

As Chapter Eight illustrated, there were examples of students applying for law courses on the basis of their specific commitments to developing knowledge and skills in the field of legal aid work; commitments that they could take forward whether as Law Centre staff or as volunteers providing pro bono sessions in the future. Law Centres had potentially important contributions to make to legal education and training for the future, providing opportunities for widening knowledge and skills as well as making students aware of professional issues and ethical dilemmas that might otherwise have passed them by, virtually unnoticed, if their training had been confined to experiences in more commercial aspects of the law. The public service ethos may be socially reproduced in such ways among individual students and volunteers, wherever they subsequently end up working.

There would seem to be implications in relation to the education and training of other professionals too. Like their counterparts in the legal profession, community workers and other community-based professionals need to be aware of the issues and dilemmas involved. And they need to have the knowledge and skills to manage the associated tensions. As previous chapters have suggested, public service professionals have to operate in a dilemmatic space in which there may be no self-evidently right thing to do (Honig, 1996). Both professionals and street-level bureaucrats experience tensions, it has been suggested, in attempting to balance colliding value systems and competing demands in the public sphere (Lipsky, 1980; Hoggett et al, 2009) under increasingly challenging circumstances in the context of public service modernisation. As previous studies have concluded, professionals such as development workers need to have the capacities to manage these tensions with reflexivity, and the ability to cope with emotions, remaining passionate as well as thoughtful (Hoggett et al, 2009). And their education and training needs to support them in developing these capabilities.

Grounds for optimism?

In summary, there were grounds for some optimism in terms of the reproduction of value commitments among the next generation. As the (then) Law Centres Federation Annual Report for 2010–11 described its position, there was also optimism more generally 'in the face of austerity' (Law Centres Federation, 2011, p 5). 'The fight for legal aid is the fight for what is just and it is a fight for our clients', the report stated. 'We must do as Law Centres have always done – fight fearlessly for our communities'; and it concluded that 'Law Centres will survive the storm'. The Annual Report of the (by then rebranded) Law Centres Network (LCN) for 2011–12 maintained this firm commitment. As the co-chairs emphasised: 'we are not defeatist. Law Centres and the LCN have been coming together throughout this year, working on ways to continue our service to our communities as they are faced with major challenges such as the impact of welfare reform' (Law Centres Network, 2011–12, p 1).

There were also grounds for optimism in terms of the development of survival strategies. Chapter Six provided illustrations of such strategies in practice, demonstrating ways of using resources more cost-effectively while continuing to provide services holistically. There were examples of Law Centres continuing to meet individuals' needs for information and advice while continuing to promote preventative approaches, for instance. And there were examples of Law Centres working collaboratively with other agencies rather than competing with them, in order to provide more comprehensive services to clients across localities. In Avon and Bristol, for example, the Advice Network coordinated services across the city and neighbouring counties, with the Law Centre providing specialist legal services. The aim was for agencies to provide a cohesive map of information, advice and advocacy, based upon collaboration with local authorities and with each other, instead of being rooted in competition for scarce resources.

Similarly, in Coventry Advice Services, Coventry had developed a joint strategy to meet clients' and communities' needs holistically as well as cost-effectively. Two-way referral relationships were developed between generalist and specialist agencies and vice versa with what was described as a very successful electronic referral system that was developed with Big Lottery funding. This illustrated the potential scope for agencies to secure additional funding on the basis of such partnership approaches.

There had been comparable developments in Nottingham, where a group of not-for-profit advice agencies had come together to form Advice Nottingham. Here too, this had improved the coverage of services as well as providing mutual support and enhanced opportunities for responding proactively in the context of funding pressures ("getting ahead of the game", as one interviewee explained it). And here too, the Law Centre had been central to these developments. The outcome had been a joined-up structure that effectively linked generalist and specialist provision, operating in more cost-effective ways without losing sight of the interests of clients and communities.

The need for continuing public sector support as part of longer-term strategies for access to justice for all

Ironically, the Cabinet Office report on *Not-for-profit advice services in England* (Cabinet Office, 2011) identified precisely such strategies as potential ways forward for advice services; strategies such as effective collaboration, early intervention and preventative work, along with greater use of telephone and web-based advice and increasing efficiency more generally. Yet this report offered only transition funding arrangements, rather than longer-term support, despite recognising the pincer effect of diminishing funding to meet increasing demands for advice services (the result, to a considerable extent, of changes in public policies towards the provision of social welfare, as the report also recognised). This was not enough, even in the short-term, let alone sufficient as a longer-term strategy to ensure access to justice for all.

The challenges and dilemmas that public service modernisation have posed for the ethos and values of staff and trustees emerged powerfully. But so too did the determination of those engaged in developing alternative responses: re-examining ways of providing services most effectively while holding on to the Law Centres' underlying ethos, developing more efficient ways of managing their operations without losing their commitment to team work, increasing the use of voluntary effort without exploiting unpaid labour, using new technologies without undermining the importance of personal face-to-face support for clients, working collaboratively in partnership with other organisations and agencies rather than via strategies based upon increasing competition.

Previous chapters have also demonstrated the human costs, including the emotional labour involved as well as the unpaid overtime and the voluntary effort that all this has required. However, it would seem unlikely that Law Centres could survive for long, without continuing public support. Despite the efforts to find ways of working smarter, to develop new forms of income generation and to attract alternatives sources of funding and volunteers, the future sustainability of Law Centres would seem to depend primarily upon underpinning by a firm foundation of public resources.

Short-term savings might be achieved by removing areas of law from the scope of legal aid, it was argued. But this would entail longer-term financial, social and human costs, with resource implications for the future. For example, Steve Hynes, director of the Legal Action Group (Hynes, 2012) reviewed the effects of cuts in social welfare law. Through a total of £280 million of cuts in funding from civil legal aid, the government estimated,[1] around 600,000 people would lose out on help with everyday civil legal problems. In making the alternative case for investment rather than cuts, the Legal Action Group highlighted the short-sightedness of such cuts in preventative and economic terms. Its research made the case that '£60m in expenditure on legal aid advice saves the state £338.65m in expenditure on other services'. The report proceeded to spell out the leverage involved: 'Put another way, one pound expenditure on legal aid saves the state around six pounds in other spending' (Hynes, 2012).

In terms of long-term savings, then, the case for cutting back on poor people's access to justice was open to question. Marketisation strategies were criticised for embodying their own internal tensions in relation to the provision of legal aid, as indeed more generally (Moorhead and Pleasance, 2003). More emphasis upon preventative strategies might prove to be far more effective. The provision of more comprehensive access to debt advice could reduce the number of cases involving rent arrears and the risk of homelessness, for instance. Improved administrative procedures could reduce the number of appeals in asylum cases and disability benefits cases – reducing the stresses experienced by those exposed to dysfunctional decision-making processes in the first place.

The criticisms of marketisation in relation to the provision of legal aid go beyond such questions of cost-effectiveness for the longer term, however. As the Scottish Government had already recognised, in contrast to the Coalition government's approach, there were wider considerations to be taken into account here. '[W]holesale reductions to scope [of legal aid] can have a damaging impact on access to justice and can have adverse consequences for other parts of the justice system as well as wider society', the LAG report concluded. Reducing legal aid to a rump service could prove to be socially destructive, and particularly so in the context of austerity. These wider implications were acknowledged even by a Conservative MP (subsequently a minister in the Ministry of Justice) when the LASPO Bill was under consideration, reflecting that 'to stem the flow of legal aid when we are in such a critical condition, amid a stifling recession, could prove devastating' (Helen Grant, MP, *Guardian*, 2 February 2011).

As the publication *Austerity justice* by Steve Hynes, director of the Legal Action Group, has argued, campaigning for access to justice must continue (Hynes, 2012). The broad coalition that campaigned for amendments to the LASPO Bill could have sown the seeds of recovery, he wrote, building support for the development of new and more comprehensive approaches to the provision of legal aid. The aim of such continued campaigning, Hynes concluded, must be to persuade the next government to map legal needs and develop a strategy for providing access to advice and support on social welfare law in England and Wales – putting right the damage that the cuts introduced by the LASPO Act were expected to cause.

Wider implications?

Access to justice has been the hallmark of the post-war welfare state and, indeed, of democratic societies more generally. 'The Law is the bedrock of a nation; it tells us who we are, what we value, who has power and who hasn't' (Kennedy, 2005b, p 3). As a lawyer who had been providing pro bono advice in a Law Centre reflected, without Law Centres people in the communities that they currently served would struggle to access justice. "What is justice", she concluded, "if people don't understand it and can't access it?" Law Centres enable people who would otherwise be unable to do so "to have access to justice and recourse to remedies". 'This is what lawyers provide to citizens, and what should be available to citizens in democratic societies under the rule of law.' This takes the discussion back to the starting point, the centrality of access to justice to debates on social welfare and social justice – the fifth pillar of the welfare state. Previous chapters have illustrated ways in which the marketisation of legal aid has been undermining people's access to justice. As Morris, among others, has argued, government perspectives on rights have been increasingly conditional (Morris, 2007), raising questions about the extent to which successive governments have been committed to one of the most fundamental features of democratic societies: equality of treatment for all citizens with universal access to the law. As previous chapters have argued, this was central to T.H. Marshall's concept of social citizenship (Marshall, 1950) backed by affordable and effective access to justice. This was an essential component of even the most limited concept of social justice: equality of treatment before the law, regardless of the ability to pay for legal advice and legal representation.

The consequences of the residualisation of legal aid emerge even more starkly when considered in the context of more expanded notions of social justice. As previous chapters have also argued, the law's relationship with the social and political order is profoundly ambiguous; the law provides safeguards against injustice, including injustices resulting from the arbitrary exercise of authority of the part of the state. Yet equal treatment before the law still tends to produce unequal outcomes when playing fields are so far from being level. This is precisely why more expanded notions of social justice underpinned the establishment of the first community Law Centres in Britain. Their remit was to go way beyond the provision of information and advice to individual clients, to include preventative policy work, advocacy and campaigning, taking up test cases, for example, as part of strategies to tackle social injustices.

Despite the pressures, there is still evidence of Law Centres' continuing commitment to these wider approaches to social justice. The Migrants' Law Project, hosted by Islington Law Centre, provides an illustration in point. Funded by donations and grants, The Migrants' Law Project represents a determined response to the loss of legal aid funding, aiming to improve the rights of migrants, refugees and asylum seekers through the use of public law. The project provides free legal advice and support to organisations working with migrants, refugees and asylum seekers, including providing them with training to enable them to negotiate more effectively with government and other relevant public bodies. And where negotiation fails, as The Migrants' Law Project's website explains, they will 'take legal action, where appropriate, to challenge unjust government policies'.[2]

As previous chapters have illustrated, these wider roles have been precisely those aspects of Law Centres' missions – challenging unjust policies in the interests of social justice agendas – that have been most effectively undermined as a result of marketisation in the provision of legal aid. Sommerlad has similarly argued, even before the changes promoted by the Coalition government, that

> the neo-liberal revolution has transformed the dialectical relationship between law and society and the social form of citizenship, and is eroding the possibility of this reformist use of the law. As a result it is likely not only to constrict the pivotal role of law in the process of participative, deliberative democracy, but its very reconstruction as a residual service plays a part in producing social exclusion. (Sommerlad, 2004, pp 367–8).

As Esping Andersen and others have argued in parallel, the (relatively) social democratic model of the welfare state that was developed in post-war Britain set out to tame, regulate or marginalise markets so as to ensure human welfare (Esping Andersen et al, 2002). This contrasts with more recent policies to promote increasing marketisation based upon envisaging service users as informed consumers. As this book has argued, there are inherent contradictions here, when such marketisation is applied to service users who are too poor to afford to pursue their rights. There are tensions and dilemmas for professionals and other public sector and community-based staff and volunteers attempting to balance their public service ethos with the requirements of organisational survival in more marketised policy contexts. And there are fundamental questions of value.

As citizens we need to be protected from arbitrary state action, just as we need to be protected from incompetence or worse on the part of service providers, including professionals such as lawyers. But this in no way implies the lack of a need for state intervention and support, despite the inevitable tensions. On the contrary, despite all the underlying limitations and biases, the state can also intervene, regulating markets and providing resources for services to promote human welfare.

There need to be powerful mechanisms to hold the state to account, of course, just as there need to be powerful mechanisms to hold professionals to account, more generally. But not via the importation of inappropriate market mechanisms, public service modernisation agendas and more recent strategies for increasing marketisation more widely.

As the evidence demonstrates, alternative ways of approaching public service reform can be effective. Services can be enhanced and service providers can be held democratically accountable to service users, would-be service users and their communities without undermining the public service ethos in the process. Marketisation is not the only, or even the most effective, way forward for the longer term, let alone the most appropriate in terms of the quality, value – and values – of social welfare and social justice.

As previous chapters have argued, there are powerful arguments to support the view that there are indeed services that are too important to be left to the vagaries of the market, such as Nussbaum's argument in relation to higher education and the humanities (Nussbaum, 2010). Commercialisation was less effective as a means of procuring human blood, in Titmuss's view, undermining reciprocity and social solidarity. Quoting from Alexander Solzhenitsyn's *Cancer ward*, Titmuss cited a discussion between two patients as to whether an economy could and should be built on an ethical basis: 'Ethics first and economics afterwards?' (Titmuss, 1970, p 208). There are contemporary resonances here. The dilemmas posed by the increasing marketisation of access to social welfare and social justice highlight Sandel's (2012) wider case for questioning: what should be the moral limits of markets?

Notes
[1] Figures from Ministry of Justice (2010), Annex A.

[2] www.themigrantslawproject.org, accessed 22 February 2013.

APPENDIX 1

Research methodology and questionnaire

The research set out to explore the impacts of public service modernisation as these agendas were being experienced and the dilemmas that were being faced by professionals and volunteers providing legal services within Law Centres. The study was planned to take place in three stages, starting with a literature review and postal/electronic survey of Law Centre staff and volunteers in England (including management committee members/trustees) to obtain benchmarks for the second stage. This second stage was originally planned to involve sets of semi-structured interviews with between 30 and 40 staff and volunteers from a sample of Law Centres. Through this more qualitative approach the research aimed to obtain in-depth understandings to complement the quantitative data from the survey. The third and final stage would then involve focus group discussions to explore preliminary findings and test conclusions before completing the research and moving into the final dissemination stage. The original timeframe envisaged that this would all be completed by 2011.

In the event however, the start of the project was delayed due to circumstances beyond the team's control. Although the research subsequently got back on track (albeit on a revised schedule, concluding in March 2012) the context was already changing rapidly. Law Centres were experiencing the impact of the implementation of funding changes including the uncertain outcomes of competitive tendering processes.

Following the election of the Coalition government in May 2010, public policy towards resourcing legal aid came under review, with new legislation being introduced, leading to further significant challenges for Law Centres, raising fundamental questions about their longer-term futures. The Law Centres' umbrella body, the LCF (subsequently renamed the Law Centres Network), estimated that a significant proportion of Law Centres would have very uncertain futures. During the research period several Law Centres closed or reduced their operations, some staff members were made redundant and further financial challenges were being anticipated in the wake of more recent public expenditure decisions. Despite this, however, the annual report for 2010–11 (Law Centres Federation, 2011) was entitled 'Weathering the Storm', testifying to the LCF's 'optimism in the face of austerity' together with their determination to safeguard services, despite these challenges. As the co-chairs' concluded 'Legal aid may be going, but our clients are not going to disappear. And nor are we' (Law Centres Federation, 2011).

This changing and increasingly problematic context required some flexibility in the research strategy, as subsequent sections outline. It also required some sensitivity. There were occasions when those who had so generously agreed to be interviewed were evidently stressed. The researchers needed to take account of the challenges facing Law Centres, including the threat of redundancies for staff and try to ensure that stress levels would in no way be exacerbated as a result of the research process itself. In the event, however, a number of those who had been interviewed subsequently commented that they had actually found it useful to have had this space – to reflect upon the dilemmas that they were facing and the strategies that were being adopted in response. The team would like to express our deep appreciation of the responsiveness of so many Law Centre staff and volunteers, despite these typically challenging circumstances.

Following consultation with the umbrella body, the LCF the questionnaire was administered electronically as well as by post with questions kept to a minimum, to take account of the then current time pressures on Law Centre staff. This appendix concludes with details of the questionnaire.

Despite some initial doubts as to the extent to which the survey would be completed at all, in these circumstances, the final total of completed questionnaires was 107. In total these replies referred to experiences in 25 different Law Centres (out of a total which was given as 55 at that time). These covered a range of Law Centres, urban and rural, large and small, including longer and more recently established ones. Appendix 2 provides details of the 43 Law Centres that were included in the research, overall (including the interviews as well as the survey responses).

At this point it should also be emphasised that the Law Centres varied considerably in terms of their histories, funding, size, organisational structures, overall focus and the areas of law that they covered (with varying administrative and funding procedures and processes). This meant that issues identified in any one Law Centre would not necessarily have applied in the same ways elsewhere. And the impact of subsequent policies and further potential changes to these may have been experienced in differing ways.

Following on from the survey, semi-structured interviews were completed, to explore the issues that had been raised, in greater depth. Appendix 3 provides the topic guides for these and subsequent semi-structured interviews. Interviews were completed with 54 people from 28 Law Centres. Of these 45 interviews were carried out on a one-to one basis. Two sets of colleagues (i.e. four individuals) chose to be interviewed together with a colleague and four further people were interviewed as a group. In addition, three other individuals were present for part of a joint interview (two of these left the group interview in order to see clients before the discussions were completed and one joined an interview with a colleague (being invited to join in order to add comments from their particular perspective, as a young volunteer).

Almost all the interviews were carried out in person, but a small number (2 interviews) were carried out over the telephone. In one case this was due to bad weather that disrupted travel plans. The other telephone interview was with a respondent who was too busy to meet but was prepared to be interviewed by telephone.

In each case, those interviewed were subsequently provided with an (edited) transcript of the discussion and offered the opportunity to point to any corrections or significant omissions. The overwhelming majority agreed that this was indeed an accurate record of the discussion. The small minority of those that did respond, added minor points of clarification, or identified comments that should not be directly quoted in case this could identify particular individuals.

The transcripts were analysed and themes identified, using NVivo software.

An Interim Report, summarising the findings from this analysis was then circulated to those who had participated and their views invited, for further discussion. The reality was, however, that although a few did express satisfaction at receiving feedback, there was very limited response, overall. This was a very challenging period for Law Centres in relation to tendering processes which might help to explain why it was difficult to engage in more detailed discussions at that stage.

Having completed this round of interviews it was decided, in addition, to interview a range of other stakeholders. This was to obtain their views on the issues in question together with their views on Law Centres' strategies for how to survive in such a challenging climate, without compromising their ethos and values. This next round of interviews provided triangulation, enabling the researchers to compare and contrast the views – and claims – of Law Centre staff and volunteers with the views of other stakeholders. More specifically this would also add depth to our understanding of the importance of and the scope for collaboration between Law Centres and other agencies, whether in the voluntary and/or statutory sectors. This was emerging as a central theme in terms of forward looking strategies for survival.

So for this second phase 58 semi-structured interviews were carried out with voluntary sector advice agencies' and voluntary sector networks' staff with knowledge and experience of working with Law Centres, local authority officers and local councillors, representatives of other funding agencies (including the LSC), lawyers with particular expertise in legal education and training and private sector lawyers, including those providing pro bono advice, together with a number of other volunteers (as this group had been relatively under-represented in the first round of interviews). Of these second round interviews 49 were face to face and 9 were telephone interviews. Here too, each person interviewed was provided with an edited draft of the discussion and invited to point to any corrections or significant omissions. Once again very few chose to make any such suggestions, the overwhelming majority simply agreeing that this was indeed an accurate record of the discussion.

In addition there were two meetings with the LCF (now the LCN) in London to explore their perspectives and then to offer interim feedback, together with a telephone interview with a member of the LCF staff with specialist knowledge of the Northern region.

In order to build up more detailed pictures of the ways in which Law Centres and other stakeholders were interacting together, this final stage of the research focused upon a limited number of geographical locations, selected to cover a range of contexts. In all, eight locations were selected for further study. Through visiting these locations on a number of occasions, the researchers were also able to develop more holistic perceptions of each context together with the operations and ethos of the Law Centres in question.

This raises the important issue of bias however. Whilst the Law Centres that were being referred to in the second phase were experiencing significant challenges, they were also amongst those that were developing some of the most apparently promising survival strategies in response. The pictures that emerged from this second phase of the research were not necessarily representative of the situation nationally, as a result, with less evidence of the type of demoralisation that had been emerging from some of the first phase of interviews (although, as it subsequently emerged, two of the Law Centres in this second phase were not just facing challenges but were actually struggling to survive).

The other significant limitation was that the research did not include interviews with service users per se. This would have involved additional resources way beyond the perimeters of this particular study. In the event, some user views were obtained; for example some volunteers and indeed some staff had previously been service users themselves. Some Law Centres had compiled user views themselves and these were made available. And some management committee members and some external stakeholders offered reflections on the user feedback that they had received. For example other advice agencies were very aware of the importance of taking account of user views, when making decisions about referring future client to Law Centres. There were, in addition, opportunities for researchers to observe some aspects of Law Centres' operations such as witnessing clients' experiences in reception, when they arrived at Law Centres seeking advice. Comments on some of these observations have been included. But overall, the views of users themselves could not be evaluated systematically, on the basis of this research.

These limitations need to be borne in mind, then. Despite these inherent limitations, however, the findings can be argued to have significance still, in their own right. They illustrate the ways in which public service modernisation agendas have been experienced by staff and volunteers and the dilemmas that they have been facing in this significant but relatively under-researched component of the Welfare State. And they provide pointers in the direction of potential ways forward, ways in which Law Centres were developing strategies to survive and to succeed in continuing to provide access to justice for disadvantaged individuals and communities – without losing sight of their professional ethos and public service values – even in the context of the challenges that they were currently facing.

The questionnaire

The impact of changes in legal aid for Law Centre staff, volunteers and management committee members: researching the challenges for Law Centres' values and ethos

The findings will be fed back and should be useful to Law Centres and the Law Centre Federation.

The study is being carried out by researchers at Goldsmiths, University of London.

The questionnaire takes 5–10 minutes to fill in.

The data will be strictly confidential and anonymous.

We very much appreciate your participation in this survey!

Section 1: You and your involvement in Law Centres

1. Which Law Centre have you been involved with, for how long and in which role? (Please start a new column after every change of Law Centre and/or role)

	Law Centre /Role (1)	Law Centre /Role (2)	Law Centre /Role (3)
Name of Law Centre			
Period of time			
Volunteer Staff member Management Committee member			
Administrator Finance Officer Community worker Solicitor Director Chair of Management committee Other:			

2. How important to you were the following factors, when you decided to work in/ give your time to a Law Centre?

	very important	fairly important	not very important	not important at all
Concern with meeting community needs for legal services				
Reasonable pay and conditions				
Challenging job				
Concern with addressing social justice issues				
Offers valuable experience/builds c.v.				
Other (please specify):				

3. Has your interest/motivation changed over time?

Yes

No

If so, in what ways?

Section 2: Current issues in Law Centres

4. Research for the Law Centres Federation has raised a number of issues and concerns about the introduction of the Unified Contract system, following the Carter report. In each case, on the basis of your own experiences, please would you identify how far you agree or disagree with the following statements, that this is indeed a problem:

	strongly agree	broadly agree	broadly disagree	strongly disagree	don't know
Standardised fixed fees underfund the complex debt, housing, employment, education, mental health and community care cases that law centres focus on.					
The Unified Contract system places increased administrative burdens on law centres.					
The scheme potentially fosters competition between local providers, putting at risk longstanding partnerships and collaborative ways of working.					
Standardised fixed fees put at risk provision and support that is specialist and challenging, encouraging Law Centres to 'cherry pick' particular types of cases (concentrating upon cases that can be resolved relatively simply, rather than providing holistic responses to the clusters of problems that are experienced by many vulnerable clients).					
Preventative work – including education work, policy work and advocacy – has been put at risk.					

5. On the basis of your experiences, do you consider that there are other issues for Law Centres, too, as a result of the introduction of the Unified Contract?

Yes

No

If so, what are these?

6. Overall, has the introduction of the Unified Contract had an effect on your own feelings about working in/volunteering in/serving on the management committee of a Law Centre?

Yes

No

If so, in what way(s)?

Section 3: Further details

Please tick all which apply:

7. Are you:

☐ Male
☐ Female

8. How would you describe your ethnicity?

☐ Black
☐ Asian
☐ Mixed Race
☐ White British
☐ White Other
☐ Other
☐ Prefer not to specify

9. Which age band are you in:

☐ Under 30
☐ 31–40
☐ 41–50
☐ 51–60
☐ Over 60

As a follow up to this survey, we shall be interviewing a sample of law centre workers, volunteers and management committee members, to explore their views in more detail.

If you might be prepared to be contacted for a follow up interview, please would you very kindly provide your name and contact details?

Law Centre:--

Name:---

Contact details (email or phone): --------------------------------

Findings

The questions about what were the current issues in Law Centres produced high levels of agreement, as it turned out. The first question asked was about the impact of standardised fixed fees. Seventy-four per cent strongly agreed with the view that standardised fees underfunded the complex debt, housing, employment, education, mental health and community care cases that Law Centres focused on, with a further 16% in broad agreement with this view.

Table 1: Standardised fixed fees underfund the complex debt, housing, employment, education, mental health and community care cases that Law Centres focus on

	Frequency	Per cent
strongly agree	79	73.8%
broadly agree	17	15.9%
broadly disagree	1	0.9%
strongly disagree	2	1.9%
don't know	2	1.9%
Missing	6	5.6%
Total	107	100%

Almost two-thirds (65%) also strongly agreed with the view that the Unified Contract system was placing increased administrative burdens on Law Centres, with a further 21% in broad agreement.

There was strong (although slightly less strong) agreement that the scheme potentially fostered competition between local providers, putting at risk long-standing partnerships and collaborative ways of working. Just under half (49%) strongly agreed, with a further 32% in broad agreement. While there was evidence of anxiety on this score, others were less concerned about this as a potential threat. The issue is examined further in Chapter Six, which explores the strategies for collaboration and partnership working that were being taken forward as part of survival plans for Law Centres for the future.

The pattern was relatively similar when it came to the issue of cherry-picking (that is, prioritising cases that would fit most readily with the fixed fee funding system), 47% strongly agreeing that this was a risk, and a further 35% being in broad agreement. Here too, there were comments pointing to the ways in which some Law Centres were taking action to avoid cherry-picking cases.

Finally, 66% of respondents strongly agreed with the view that preventative work, including public legal education, policy and advocacy work was being put at risk, with a further 22% in broad agreement.

Table 2: With the introduction of fixed fees preventative work – including education work, policy work and advocacy – has been put at risk

	Frequency	Per cent
strongly agree	71	66.4%
broadly agree	24	22.4%
broadly disagree	1	0.9%
strongly disagree	3	2.8%
don't know	2	1.9%
Missing	6	5.6%
Total	107	100%

Respondents were then asked if there were any other issues for Law Centres as a result of the introduction of the Unified Contract. In total just under two-thirds (63%) thought that there were.

The following comments illustrate these.

"Payment at the end of a case and the fixed fees system has eroded reserves, putting the survival of the Law Centre at threat, causing de-motivation within staff and in fact staff losses and cuts in terms and conditions", according to one respondent. "Not drawing down enough funding to cover costs and salaries", added another.

The ways in which the Unified Contract operated were cited here, as well as the financial impacts of the fixed fees system. One respondent wrote as follows: "Feel worn down by the bureaucracy of casework. Like being on a treadmill." "LSC issues very frustrating – reduces motivation", added another. "Hitting targets becomes a big driving factor even though I don't like this aspect of my job", wrote a third. "The emphasis has to be on maximising income, by meeting individual targets. This narrows what one can do. The workplace has become more pressurised. There is much less opportunity to provide a holistic service."

"Pressures to close cases prematurely", wrote another respondent. "Law Centres waste time and money due to LSC administrative incompetence/bureaucracy", added another. "Ultimately clients will suffer as they will effectively be deprived of access to justice, most clients are vulnerable and poor", reflected yet another. "Generally the measure of success has become driven by achievement of targets rather than benefits to clients. This is demoralising and can be divisive to the staff team", was the verdict of a further respondent, summarising their views on the impact of public service modernisation as exemplified by the Carter reforms. As another respondent put this, "it emphasises targets and, as has been evidenced in other services, it is possible to meet targets whilst providing a service that serves no-one adequately".

Broadly, these findings were consistent with many of the concerns that had been identified in the literature review, focusing upon the changes that had accompanied the introduction of the Carter reforms and the administrative systems involved in LSC-supported provision since then. The responses were by no means unanimous, however. For example, there were some differing views on the extent to which collaborative work and partnership working were being put at risk. (The interviews subsequently provided evidence that this risk had not actually materialised in some cases: there were examples where increased partnership working had been developed between Law Centres, other advice agencies and other service providers, as Chapter Six discusses in more detail.)

There were also comments that indicated that Law Centres should not attribute all their problems to the LSC. "I think it is mistaken to attribute all our ills to the LSC", a respondent commented, going on to refer to reductions in other funding sources and concluding that it was "partly also Law Centres' failure to adapt our mission and message to modern conditions". The interviews provided fuller evidence on this topic too, including reflections on some of the dilemmas inherent in managing the potential tensions between modernising and becoming more business-like, on the one hand, and fears of the possible loss of mission, on the other, as Chapter Eight explores in more detail.

Comparisons by gender

The responses of the 56 women who completed the survey differed very little, if at all, from the men's responses. There were only two tables where there seemed to be some minor differences. One of these tables related to responses to the question about whether or not the Carter reforms were leading to increasing competition, rather than collaboration between providers. Here women were rather less likely to think that this was the case; indicating, perhaps, that women were more committed to the values of collaboration and more determined to continue to collaborate with colleagues? This may or may not have been the case.

Table 3: The scheme potentially fosters competition between local providers, putting at risk longstanding partnerships and collaborative ways of working.

	Absolute		Per cent	
	male	female	male	female
strongly agree	22	29	50%	53%
broadly agree	19	16	43%	29%
broadly disagree	0	6	0%	11%
strongly disagree	0	1	0%	2%
don't know	3	3	7%	5%
Total	44	55	100%	100%

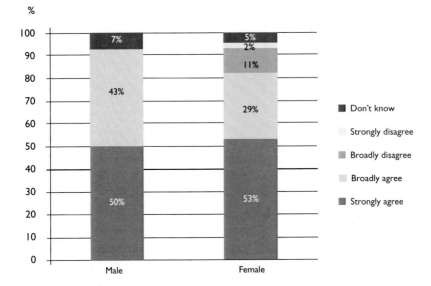

When it came to the issue of motivation, the differences seemed, if anything, to be counter-intuitive. Women were slightly more likely than men to consider that pay and conditions were important as motivating factors. Again, the reasons for this can only be speculated about.

Table 4: How important to you were reasonable pay and conditions, when you decided to work in/give your time to a Law Centre?

	Absolute		Per cent	
	male	female	male	female
very important	11	15	26%	28%
fairly important	19	28	44%	52%
not very important	12	6	28%	11%
not important at all	1	5	2%	9%
Total	43	54	100%	100%

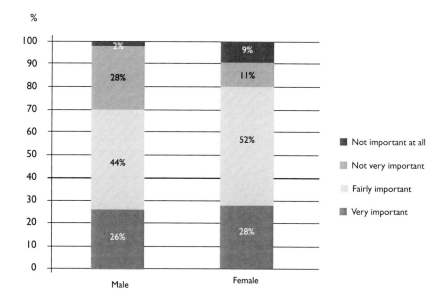

APPENDIX 2

Law Centres included

Avon and Bristol Law Centre
Barnet Law Centre
Birmingham Law Centre
Brent Community Law Centre
Bury Law Centre
Cambridge House
Camden Community Law Centre
Chesterfield Law Centre
Coventry Law Centre
Cross Street Law Centre
Croydon Law Centre
Cumbria Law Centre
Derby Citizens Advice and Law Centre
Gloucester Law Centre
Greenwich Law Centre
Hackney Community Law Centre
Hammersmith and Fulham Law Centre
Harehills Law Centre
Hillingdon Law Centre
Islington Law Centre
Kent Law Clinic
Wiltshire Law Centre
Wythenshawe Law Centre

Lambeth Law Centre
Leeds Law Centre
Luton Law Centre
Newcastle Law Centre
North Kensington Law Centre
Nottingham Law Centre
Oldham Law Centre
Paddington Law Centre
Plumstead Law Centre
Rochdale Law Centre
Saltley and Nechells Law Centre
Sheffield Law Centre
South Manchester Law Centre
South West London Law Centre
Southwark Law Centre
Streetwise Community Law Centre
Surrey Law Centre
Tower Hamlets Law Centre
Vauxhall Law Centre
Wandsworth and Merton Law Centre

APPENDIX 3

Topic guides for semi-structured interviews

Law Centres

(1st round interviews)

1. Explore the participant's motivation for becoming involved with Law Centres (whether as a paid worker, volunteer or management committee member).
2. Invite participant to summarise the history of their involvement (e.g. having started to become involved as a volunteer/or client).
3. Has the motivation for their involvement changed over time? If so, in what ways and why?
4. Does the Law Centre(s) have a particular ethos? If so, how would they describe this? How important is this for them?
5. How (if at all) might this relate to wider debates about the future of the public service ethos more generally?
6. Invite the participant to comment more specifically on their views on the impact of recent policy changes. How have these changes affected them, both in practical ways and in terms of their motivation and commitment?
7. How have these changes been managed/coped with? And how has the participant been managing these changes and their feelings about them?
8. Are there tensions/professional dilemmas involved here? If so, how does the participant cope with these/with what coping strategies and resources to draw upon (both internal resources and external resources, including sharing tensions with colleagues/former colleagues/friends)?
9. More generally, how does the participant see the future of Law Centres, taking account of differing/contradictory policy objectives e.g. for enabling the most disadvantaged to become active consumers of public services whilst also saving money on legal services – and for promoting 'new and more accountable forms of professionalism' rather than de-professionalisation?
10. How does the participant see their own future in Law Centres – or elsewhere?

Other stakeholders (such as local authorities)

(2nd round interviews)

1. How have you/your organisation come to be supporting/resourcing/working in collaboration with/in partnership with the Law Centre (initial motivation/ and continuing motivation)?
2. How would you describe your organisation's particular relationship with the Law Centre? Has this changed over time? If so in what ways and why? Have there been differences of perspective (e.g. between councillors and officers)?
3. How would you describe the Law Centre's particular ethos – and its particular contributions to local communities – and to access to justice more widely? (commenting on Law Centres' own views on their specific roles and contribution including):
   - reaching particularly disadvantaged groups/communities regardless of ability to pay for access to justice
   - providing holistic services to individuals/communities/addressing related issues such as housing/benefits/immigration holistically
   - undertaking preventative work through public legal education/training
   - negotiating e.g. working with public authorities to address individual/ collective concerns in preventative ways
   - undertaking policy work
   - providing specialist advice/support/training to other agencies e.g. CABs and other advice services as part of holistic approach to provision within localities
   - taking up test cases in welfare and related areas of law

Anything else?

1. How would you describe/summarise the current and forthcoming challenges to Law Centres including potential changes to the availability of legal aid?
2. What in your view might be relevant ways forward/which types of approaches might be appropriate to meet these challenges, building upon Law Centres' particular areas of expertise – and without losing Law Centres' particular ethos?
3. More specifically how far do you think that volunteering could provide solutions/what if any might be the limitations to volunteering in this context?
4. Any other comments/reflections?

Volunteers

(2nd round interviews)

1. How have you come to be volunteering/still volunteering (initial motivation/ and continuing motivation)?
2. How would you describe your particular contribution to the Law Centre?
3. How would you describe the Law Centre's particular ethos – and its particular contributions to local communities – and to access to justice more widely? (commenting on Law Centres' own views on their specific roles and contribution including):
   - reaching particularly disadvantaged groups/communities regardless of ability to pay for access to justice
   - providing holistic services to individuals/communities/addressing related issues such as housing/benefits/immigration holistically
   - undertaking preventative work through public legal education/training
   - negotiating e.g. with public authorities to address individual/collective concerns in preventative ways
   - undertaking policy work
   - providing specialist advice/support/training to other agencies e.g. CABs as part of holistic approach to provision within localities
   - taking up test cases in welfare and related areas of law

Anything else?

1. How would you describe/summarise the current and forthcoming challenges to Law Centres?
2. What in your view might be relevant ways forward/which types of approaches might be appropriate to meet these challenges without losing Law Centres' particular ethos and contributions?
3. More specifically how far do you think that volunteering could provide solutions/what if any might be the limitations to volunteering in this context?
4. Any other comments/reflections?

References

Abel, R. (2003) *English lawyers between market and state*, Oxford: Oxford University Press.

Abel-Smith, B. and Titmuss, K. (eds) (1974) *Social policy*, London: Allen and Unwin.

Abel-Smith, B. and Townsend, P. (1965) *The poor and the poorest*, London: Bell.

Abel-Smith, B., Zander, M. and Brooke, R. (1973) *Legal problems and the citizen*, London: Heinemann.

Advice Services Alliance (2005) *Making legal rights a reality: The Advice Services Alliance's response to the Legal Services Commission's consultation paper*, London: Advice Services Alliance.

Balloch, S. and Taylor, M. (eds) (2001) *Partnership working*, Bristol: Policy Press.

Banks, S. (2004) *Ethics, accountability and the social professions*, Basingstoke: Palgrave Macmillan.

Banks, S. and Gallagher, A. (2009) *Ethics in professional life*, Basingstoke: Palgrave Macmillan.

Barnes, M. and Prior, D. (2009) *Subversive citizens*, Bristol: Policy Press.

Bauman, Z. (2011) *Collateral damage: Social inequalities in a global age*, Cambridge: Polity Press.

Benington, J. and Moore, M. (eds) (2010) *Public value: Theory and practice*, Basingstoke: Palgrave Macmillan.

Beresford, P. and Turner, G. (1997) *It's our welfare*, Report of the Citizens' Commission on the Future of the Welfare State, London: National Institute of Social Work.

Bindman, G. (2002) 'What made me a legal aid lawyer?', *Journal of Law and Society*, vol 29, no 3, pp 510–20.

Blackledge, P. (2012) *Marxism and Ethics*, Albany, New York: SUNY.

Blair, A. (2001), quoted in House of Commons Public Administration Select Committee on the Public Service Ethos, Seventh Report of Session 2001-02 Volume 1, London: Stationery Office.

Bocker, H.J. and Overgaard, H.O. (1982) 'Japanese quality circles: a managerial response to the productivity problem', *Management International Review*, vol 22, no 2, pp 13–19.

Bonoli, G. (1997) 'Classifying welfare states; a two-dimension approach', *Journal of Social Policy*, vol 26, no 3, pp 351–72.

Boyle, D. (2011) 'The pitfalls and perils of payment by results', *Local Economy*, vol 26, pp 627–34.

Brennan, M. (2009) 'Steering teachers: working to control the feminized profession of education', *Journal of Sociology*, vol 45, no (4) pp 339–59.

Bryson, V. and Deery, R. (2011) 'Social justice and time: the impact of public-sector reform on the work of midwives in the National Health Service', in V. Bryson and P. Fisher (eds) *Redefining social justice*, Manchester: Manchester University Press, pp 99–118.

Bryson, V. and Fisher, P. (2011) 'Introduction', in V. Bryson and P. Fisher (eds) *Redefining social justice*, Manchester: Manchester University Press, pp 1-16.

Buckingham, H. (2009) 'Competition and contracts in the voluntary sector: exploring the implications for homelessness service providers in Southampton', *Policy and Politics*, vol 37, no 2, pp 235–54.

Burchardt, T. and Craig, G. (2008) 'Introduction', in G. Craig, T. Burchardt and D. Gordon (eds) *Social justice and public policy*, Bristol: Policy Press, pp 3-5.

Burdett, J. (2004) *Professional accountability and community control: The governance of community Law Centres in England*, unpublished PhD thesis, London: London School of Economics.

Cabinet Office (2011) *Not-for-profit advice services in England*, London: Cabinet Office.

Cairns, B., Harris, M. and Hutchinson, R. (2006) *Servants of the community or agents of government*, London: Institute for Voluntary Action Research.

Callinicos, A. (2001) 'Having your cake and eating it', *Historical Materialism*, vol 9, pp 169–95.

Clarke, J. (2004) 'Dissolving the public realm? The logics and limits of neo-liberalism', *Journal of Social Policy*, vol 33, no 1, pp 27–48.

Clarke, J. and Newman, J. (1997) *The managerial state: Power, politics and ideology in the remaking of welfare*, London: Sage

Clarke, J., Smith, N. and Vidler, E. (2006) 'The indeterminacy of choice: political and organisational implications', *Social Policy and Society*, vol 5, no 3, pp 327–36.

Cohn, E.J. (1943) 'Legal aid for the poor: A study in comparative law and legal reform', *Law Quarterly Review*, vol 59, pp 250-71.

Collins, R. (1990) 'Market closure and the conflict theory of the professions', in M. Burrage and R. Torstenndahl (eds) *Professions in theory and history: Rethinking the study of the professions*, London: Sage, pp 24–44.

Commission on Social Justice (1994) *Social justice: Strategies for national renewal*, London: Verso.

Cookson, G. (2011) *Unintended consequences: The cost of the government's legal aid reforms: a report for the Law Society of England and Wales*, London: King's College.

Cooper, A. (2008) 'Welfare: dead, dying or just transubstantiated?', *Soundings*, vol 38, pp 29–41.

Council on Social Action (2009) *Time well-spent: The importance of the one-to-one relationship between advice workers and their clients*, London: Council on Social Action.

Craig, G., Atkin, K., Chattoo, S. and Flynn, R. (2012) *Understanding 'race' and ethnicity*, Bristol: Policy Press.

Crouch, C. (2011) 'Privates, publics and values', in J. Benington and M. Moore (eds) *Public value: Theory and practice*, Basingstoke: Palgrave Macmillan, pp 52–73.

Crowley, M., Tope, D., Chamberlain, L. and Hodson, R. (2010) 'Neo-Taylorism at work: occupational change in the post-Fordist era', *Social Problems*, vol 57, no 3, pp 421–47.

Deakin, N. (1993) 'Privatism and partnership in urban policy', in C. Jones (ed.) *New perspectives on the welfare state in Europe*, London: Routledge, pp 84–107.

Donaldson, L. (1990) 'The ethereal hand: organizational economics and management theory', *Academy of Management Review*, vol 15, no 3, pp 369–81.

Doonan, K. (2009) *New capitalism*, Cambridge: Polity Press.

Dorling, D. (2010) *Injustice: Why social inequality persists*, Bristol: Policy Press.

Downs, A. (1966) *Inside bureaucracy*, Boston, MA: Little, Brown and Co.

Doyal, L. and Gough, I. ((1991) *A theory of human need*, Basingstoke: Macmillan.

Drakeford, M. (2008) 'Going private?', in M. Powell (ed) *Modernising the welfare state: The Blair legacy*, Bristol: Policy Press, pp 161–78.

du Gay, P. (2000) 'Entrepreneurial governance and public management: the anti-bureaucrats', in J., Clarke S. Gewirtz and E. McLaughlin (eds) *New managerialism, new welfare?*, London: Sage Publications, pp 62–81.

Dworkin, R. (1981) 'What is equality?', *Philosophy and Public Affairs*, vol 10, pp 283–345.

Entwistle, T. and Martin, S. (2005) 'From competition to collaboration in public service delivery: a new agenda for research', *Public Administration*, vol 83, no 1, pp 233–42.

Esping Andersen, G. (1990) *Three worlds of welfare capitalism*, Princeton NJ: Princeton University Press.

Esping Andersen, G. (1999) *Social foundations of postindustrial economies*, Oxford: Oxford University Press.

Esping Andersen, G., with Gallie, D., Hemerijck, A. and Myles, J. (2002) *Why we need a new welfare state*, Oxford: Oxford University Press.

Evans, T. (2010) *Professional discretion in welfare services*, Farnham: Ashgate.

Felts, A. and Jos, P. (2000) 'Time and space: the origins and implications of the new public management', *Administrative Theory and Praxis*, vol 22, no 3, pp 519–33.

Finch, J. and Groves, D. (eds) (1983) *A labour of love: Women, work and caring*, London: Routledge and Kegan Paul.

Finlayson, A. (2003) *Making sense of New Labour*, London: Lawrence and Wishart.

Flynn, N. (2007) *Public management*, London: Sage.

Fraser, N. (2008) *Adding insult to injury*, London: Verso.

Glendinning, C., Powell, M. and Rummery, K. (eds) (2002) *Partnerships, New Labour and the governance of welfare*, Bristol: Policy Press.

Hale, B. (2011) *Equal access to justice in the Big Society*, Sir Henry Hodge Memorial Lecture, 27 June 2011, London: The Law Society.

Hansen, O. (2006) *CLACs and CLANs: A new reality? Legal action feature*, London: Legal Action Group.

Harris, M. (2010) *Business and the voluntary sector: Foundations for a research agenda*, London: Institute for Voluntary Action Research.

Healy, K. (2009) 'A case of mistaken identity: the social welfare professions and new public management', *Journal of Sociology*, vol 45, no 4, pp 401–18.

Hochshild, A. (1983) *The managed heart: The commercialisation of human feeling*, Berkeley, CA: University of California Press.

Hoggett, P. (1996) 'New modes of control in the public service', *Public Administration*, vol 74, pp 9–32.

Hoggett, P., Mayo, M. and Miller, C. (2009) *The dilemmas of development work*, Bristol: Policy Press.

Honig, B. (1996) 'Difference, dilemmas and the politics of home', in S. Benhabib (ed) *Democracy and difference: Contesting the boundaries of the political*, Princeton, NJ: Princeton University Press.

Hood, C. (1991) 'A public management for all seasons?' *Public Administration*, vol 69, no 1, pp 3–19.

House of Commons Public Administration Select Committee (2002) *The public service ethos*, London: The Stationery Office.

Hugman, R. (2005) *New approaches in ethics for the caring professions*, Basingstoke: Palgrave Macmillan.

Hynes, S. (2012) *Austerity justice*, London: Legal Action Group.

Hynes, S. and Robins, J. (2009) *The justice gap: Whatever happened to legal aid?* London: Legal Action Group.

James, D. and Killick, E. (2010) 'Ethical dilemmas? UK immigration, legal aid funding reform and caseworkers', *Anthropology Today*, vol 26, pp 13–15.

John, P. and Johnson, M. (2008) 'Is there still a public service ethos?', in A. Park, J. Thompson, M. Phillips, M. Johnson and E. Cleary (eds) (2008) *British social attitudes: The 24th report*, London: Sage, pp 105–22.

Johnson, J. (1999) 'Justice and reform: a quarter century later', in F. Regan, A. Paterson, T. Goriely and D. Fleming (eds) *The transformation of legal aid*, Oxford: Oxford University Press, pp 205-32.

Kail, A. and Abercrombie, R. (2013) *Collaborating for impact*, London: NPC and Impetus.

Kennedy, H. (2009) 'Preface', in S. Hynes, and J. Robins (eds) (2009) *The justice gap*, London: Legal Action Group.

Kennedy, H. (2005a) *Eve was framed*, London: Vintage.

Kennedy, H. (2005b) *Just law: The changing face of justice and why it matters to us all*, London: Vintage.

Kilwein, J. (1999) 'The decline of the legal services corporation: "It's ideological, stupid!"', in F. Regan, A. Paterson, T. Goriely and D. Fleming (eds) *The transformation of legal aid*, Oxford: Oxford University Press, pp 41-63.

Kolthoff, E., Huberts, H. and van den Heuvel, H. (2007) 'The ethics of new public management: is integrity at stake?', *Public Administration Quarterly*, vol 30, no 4, pp 399–439.

Law Centres Federation (2011) *Weathering the storm: Annual report 2010/11*, London: Law Centres Federation (now Law Centres Network), www.lawcentres.org.uk.

Law Centres Federation Evaluation Framework Team (1988) *Questions of value*, London: Law Centres Federation Evaluation Framework Team.

Law Centres Network (2011–12) *Annual report: Forging lasting networks*, London: Law Centres Network, www.lawcentres.org.uk.

Law Society (2006) *What price justice?*, London: Law Society.

Le Grand, J. (2003) *Motivation, agency and public policy*, Oxford: Oxford University Press.

Le Grand, J. and Bartlett, W. (1993) 'Introduction' and 'The theory of quasi-markets', in J. Le Grand and W. Bartlett (eds) *Quasi-markets and social policy*, Basingstoke: Macmillan, pp 1–12 and 13–34.

Lee, P. and Raban, C. (1988) *Welfare theory and social policy*, London: Sage.

Legal Action Group (2012) *Social welfare law: What the public wants from civil legal aid*, London: Legal Action Group.

Lipsky, M. (1980) *Street-level bureaucracy: Dilemmas of the individual in public service*, New York: Russell Sage.

Lister, R. (1996) 'Citizenship engendered', in D. Taylor (ed) *Critical social policy*, London: Sage, pp 168–74.

London Edinburgh Weekend Return Group (1980) *In and against the state*, London: Pluto.

Lord Carter of Coles (2006) *Lord Carter's review of legal aid procurement – legal aid: a market-based approach to reform*, London: House of Lords.

LSC (Legal Services Commission) (2005) *Making legal rights a reality: The Legal Services Commission's strategy for the Community Legal Service*. Volume One: A consultation paper, London: Legal Services Commission.

LSC (2011) *Legal Services Commission response to Cabinet Office's Green Paper on 'Modernising Commissioning'*, London: Legal Services Commission.

Makepeace, A. (2009) 'Size matters when you take on civil legal aid work, if you want to make a profit', *Law Society Gazette*, 10 December.

Manson, J. (2012) 'Introduction', in *Public services on the brink*, Exeter: Imprint Academic.

Marris, P. and Rein, M. (1967) *Dilemmas of social reform*, New York: Atherton Press.

Marshall, T.H. (1950) *Citizenship and social class*, Cambridge: Cambridge University Press.

Milbourne, L. (2009) 'Remodelling the third sector: advancing collaboration or competition in community-based initiatives?', *Journal of Social Policy*, vol 38, pp 277–97.

Milbourne, L. and Cushman, M. (2013) 'From the third sector to the Big Society: how changing UK government policies have eroded third sector trust', *Voluntas*, vol 24, no 2, pp 485–508.

Milburn, A. (2001) *Report on the Commission on Building Public–Private Partnerships*, London: Institute for Public Policy Research.

Ministry of Justice (2010) *Proposals for the reform of legal aid in England and Wales*, Consultation paper, London: Ministry of Justice.

Ministry of Justice (2011a) *Legal aid reform in England and Wales: The government response*, London: Ministry of Justice.

Moorhead, R. and Pleasance, P. (2003) 'Access to justice after universalism: introduction', *Journal of Law and Society*, vol 30, no 1, pp 1–10.

Morris, L. (2007) 'New Labour's community of rights: welfare, immigration and asylum', *International Social Policy*, vol 36, no 1, pp 39–57.

Murray, U. (2012) 'Local government and the meaning of publicness', in J. Manson (ed) *Public services on the brink*, Exeter: Imprint Academic.

NEF Consulting (2008) *The socio-economic value of law centres*, London: New Economics Foundation.

NEF Consulting (2009) *Review of the impact of the Unified Contract on Law Centres*, London: New Economics Foundation.

NEF Consulting (2010a) *Law Centres Federation: what is real value?*, London: New Economics Foundation.

NEF Consulting (2010b) *Outcomes in advice*, London: New Economics Foundation.

Newman, J. (2000) 'Beyond the New Public Management? Modernizing public services', in J. Clarke, S. Gewirtz and E. McLaughlin (eds) *New managerialism, new welfare?*, London: Sage, pp 45–61.

Newman, J. and Clarke, J. (2009) *Publics, politics and power*, London: Sage Publications.

Newman, S. and Lawler, J. (2009) 'Managing healthcare under new public management: a Sisyphean challenge for nursing', *Journal of Sociology*, vol 45, no 4, pp 419–32.

Newman, J., Glendinning, C. and Hughes, M. (2008) 'Beyond modernisation? Social care and the transformation of welfare governance', *Journal of Social Policy*, vol 34, no 4, pp 531–57.

Nussbaum, M. (2003) 'Capabilities as fundamental entitlements: Sen and social justice', *Feminist Economics*, vol 9, no 2–3, pp 33–59.

Nussbaum, M. (2010) *Not for profit: Why democracy needs the humanities*, Princeton, NJ: Princeton University Press.

Page, R. (2007) *Revisiting the welfare state*, Maidenhead: Open University Press.

Paterson, A. and Sherr, A. (1999) 'Quality legal services: the dog that did not bark', in F. Regan, A. Paterson, T. Goriely and D. Fleming (eds) *The transformation of legal aid*, Oxford; Oxford University Press, pp 233–58 (reprinted 2002).

Perry, J. and Hondeghem, A. (2008) *Public service motivation: State of science and art*, Oxford: Oxford University Press.

Perry, J. and Wise, L. (1990) 'The motivational bases of public service', *Public Administration Review*, vol 50, no 3, pp 267–373.

Phillips, A. (2002) 'Multiculturalism, univeralism, and the claims of democracy', in M. Molyneux and S. Razavi (eds) *Gender justice, development and rights*, Oxford: Oxford University Press.

Piachaud, D. (2008) 'Social justice and public policy: a social policy perspective', in G. Craig, T. Burchardt and D. Gordon (eds) *Social justice and public policy*, Bristol: Policy Press, pp 33–51.

Pollitt, C. (1990) *Managerialism and the public services: The Anglo-American experience*, Oxford/Cambridge, MA: Blackwell Scientific Publications.

Powell, M. (2008) 'Introduction: modernising the welfare state', in M. Powell (ed) *Modernising the welfare state*, Bristol: Policy Press.

Power, M. (1999) *The audit society: Rituals of verification*, Oxford: Oxford University Press.

Rawls, J. (1971) *A theory of justice*, Cambridge MA: Harvard University Press.

Regan, F., Paterson, A., Goriely, T. and Fleming, D. (eds) (1999) *The transformation of legal aid*, Oxford: Oxford University Press (reprinted 2002).

Ross, J.E. and Ross, W.C. (1982) *Japanese quality circles and productivity*, VA, USA: Reston Publishing.

Sandel, M. *(1998) Liberalism and the limits of justice*, 2nd edn, Cambridge: Cambridge University Press.

Sandel, M. (2012) *What money can't buy*, New York: Farrar, Straus and Giroux.

Sanderson, P. and Sommerlad, H. (2011) 'Colonising law for the poor: access to justice in the new regulatory state', in V. Bryson and P. Fisher (eds) *Redefining social justice: New Labour rhetoric and reality*, Manchester: Manchester University Press, pp 178–200.

Schofield, T. (2009) 'Gendered organizational dynamics: the elephant in the room for Australian allied health workforce policy and planning?', *Journal of Sociology*, vol 45, no 4, pp 383–400.

Scott-Moncrieff, L. (2010) 'Virtual against traditional: contrasting legal aid business models', *Law Society Gazette*, 11 March.

Seldon, A. (2004) *Blair*, London: The Free Press.

Sen, A. (1992) *Inequality re-examined*, Oxford: Oxford University Press.

Sen, A. (1993) 'Capability and well-being', in M. Nussbaum and A. Sen (eds) *The quality of life*, Oxford: Clarendon Press, pp 30–53.

Smith, P. (1999) 'Logging emotions: a logbook of personal reflections', *Soundings*, vol 11, pp 128–37.

Smith, R. (1997) 'Clinics in a cold climate: Community Law Centres in England and Wales', *Osgoode Hall Law Journal*, vol 35, pp 895–924.

Sommerlad, H. (2001) 'I've lost the plot: an everyday story of legal aid lawyers', *Journal of Law and Society*, vol 28, no 3, pp 335–60.

Sommerlad, H. (2004) 'Some reflections on the relationship between citizenship, access to justice, and the reform of legal aid', *Journal of Law and Society*, vol 31, no 3, pp 345–68.

Sommerlad, H. (2008) 'Reflections on the reconfiguration of access to justice', *International Journal of the Legal Profession*, vol 15, no 3, pp 179–93.

Sommerlad, H. (2010) 'The implementation of quality initiatives and the new public management in the legal aid sector in England and Wales: bureaucratisation, stratification and surveillance', *International Journal of the Legal Profession*, vol 6, no 3, pp 311–43.

Standing, G. (2011) *The precariat*, London: Bloomsbury.

Stephenson, M.-A. and Harrison, J. (2011) *Unravelling equality*, Warwick: University of Warwick Law School.

Steele, J. (1999) *Wasted values: Harnessing the commitment of public managers*, London: Public Management Foundation.

Stoney, C. (2001) 'Strategic management or strategic Taylorism? A case study into change within UK local authority', *The International Journal of Public Sector Management*, vol 14, no 1, pp 27–42.

Stuffins, C. (2011) 'Working with the voluntary sector: councils encourage collaboration', *Guardian*, 11 January.

Thatcher, M. (1993) *The Downing Street years*, London: Harper Collins.

Thompson, E.P. (1967) 'Time, work-discipline, and industrial capitalism', *Past and Present*, vol 38, no 1, pp 56–97.

Titmuss, R. (1960) *The irresponsible society*, London: Fabian Society.

Titmuss, R. (1968) *Commitment to welfare*, London: Allen and Unwin.

Titmuss, R. (1970) *The gift relationship: From human blood to social policy*, London: Allen and Unwin.

Townsend, P. (1979) *Poverty in the United Kingdom*, Harmondsworth: Penguin.

Ungerson, C. (ed.) (1990) *Gender and caring*, London: Harvester Wheatsheaf.

Wedderburn, D. (1965) 'Facts and theories of the welfare state', in R. Miliband and J. Saville (eds) *The Socialist Register*, London: Merlin, pp 127–45.

Whitfield, D. (2006) *New Labour's attack on public services*, Nottingham: Spokesman.

Wilding, P. (1982) *Professional power and social welfare*, London: Routledge and Kegan Paul.

Williams, F. (1989) *Social policy*, Cambridge: Polity Press.

Williams, I. (2006) *What does competition and collaboration mean in the VCS?*, London: National Council for Voluntary Organisations Resource Paper.

Wolff, J. (2008) 'Social justice and public policy: a view from political philosophy', in G. Craig, T. Burchardt and D. Gordon (eds) *Social justice and public policy*, Bristol: Policy Press, pp 17–31.

Young, I.M. (2008) 'Structural injustice and the politics of difference', in G. Craig, T. Burchardt and D. Gordon (eds) *Social justice and public policy*, Bristol: Policy Press, pp 77–101.

Zemans, F. and Thomas, A. (1999) 'Can community clinics survive? A comparative study of Law Centres in Australia, Ontario and England', in F. Regan, A. Paterson, T. Goriely and D. Fleming (eds) *The transformation of legal aid*, Oxford: Oxford University Press.

Index

Please note: LCs refers to Law Centres